WHAT'S THE WORST THAT COULD HAPPEN?

RENA KILGANNON

How women entrepreneurs succeed: they ask, risk, and put it all on the line

First published by Kilgannon Group, LLC
ISBN 978-0-9893728-6-2
Library of Congress Control Number: 2014908936

Printed in the United States of America

Kilgannon Group, LLC
1266 W. Paces Ferry Road, Suite 246
Atlanta, GA 30327-2306

www.renakilgannon.com

To my aunt Carol Ladenheim, for creating this dream,

and

to my husband, Bob Kilgannon, for seeing me through this journey

and for making all my dreams come true.

CONTENTS

ACKNOWLEDGEMENTS

I could not have written this book without the support of my family and friends, most especially those who encouraged me along the way. To my book coach and "sherpa," Anita Paul, your belief in this endeavor, along with your patience and diligence, has been an enormous help. I am very grateful.

To the women who generously gave their time and support—A. Lizz Patrick, Ellen Dracos Lemming, Stacy Williams, and Mitzi Moore—your stories and the paths you have taken inspire me beyond words. To my other female entrepreneur pals who have advised and listened during this process, thank you so much. Deep appreciation goes to the women who worked with me at the very beginning and have stayed close to me throughout: Ellen, Stacy, Lisa, Kristin, Julie, and Janet.

To my family, friends, and mentors—Bob Kilgannon, Michael Reineck, Rick McReynolds, Don and Heidi Schultz, Michael Hammond, Julie Pigott, Harley Griffiths, and Tim Williams—I could not have done any of this without your love, friendship, and counsel over the years.

Many thanks go to Debbie Wetherhead and Susan Weissman for agreeing to read the complete manuscript in its first iteration. I hope you notice your influence as you read the final book. Your input and friendship mean a lot to me.

Great appreciation and love go to my parents, Charles and Gloria Klein. Both had immense faith in me, and my love for them knows no bounds. I miss them but will always be thankful for how they inspired me. Love to SK.

INTRODUCTION

"What's the worst that could happen?
Everyone turned me down; big deal."
J K. Rowling

When I started my company 25 years ago, I was fulfilling a childhood dream. I knew when I was very young that I wanted to be in charge of a company. I had no idea at the time what it would look like; I had a feeling that being in charge of something I owned was probably the most glamorous job I could have.

I ended up in the advertising business. I started and ran my own agency, The Kilgannon Group, in Atlanta, Georgia, for 25 years. I had several business partners, had sales in the millions of dollars, and built a solid reputation. For the first nine years, I was the sole owner. As the business grew, I grew smart enough to realize I needed help from people with more experience and knowledge than I had in certain areas. I took on three partners starting in 1997. All three were instrumental to the continued growth we experienced.

Being in business was the right choice for me. I wanted to be involved in a creative enterprise, but there was a time that I was torn between performing in theatre and running my own business. I quickly realized where my strengths lie; I love business and all things to do with creativity, so advertising is where I ended up. As for my life in theatre, I'll just say it was fun while it lasted, and I'm glad I didn't quit my day job.

Over the years, I've taken the hard knocks, achieved lots of successes, and learned a few things. My takeaways have given me a different view on life, allowed me to see who I really am, showed me the power of giving and receiving help, and most of all, taught me that life goes on even after experiencing the worst thing. I'm happy to share some of what I've learned to help other women in business and aspiring entrepreneurs.

I interviewed several women entrepreneurs for this book, all from a range of backgrounds and different business sectors. A few of them, like me, wanted to run their own business since they were young. The women whose comments you'll read in this book are those who had an idea, wanted something more for themselves, took a chance, experienced some bumps and bruises, and made it work.

I consider these women—and other female business owners—mavericks, the exceptions to the rule. We are not special in the way that suggests we had an unfair advantage that pushed us forward on our journeys. At the end of day, we take risks that others are reluctant to take and that puts us into the broad category of the entrepreneur. Without exception, we, and many others, share the humble, sometimes ridiculous mantra that has enabled us to take one more step towards our goals: What's the worst that could happen?

IT'S
SUE CARROLL'S
1 | FAULT

■ ■ ■ ■ ■

*"We never know which lives we influence,
or when, or why."*
Stephen King

■ ■ ■ ■ ■

Everyone is influenced by someone. In my case, one of my mother's sisters, Carol Ladenheim, was the one who made everything seem special. She owned a business in New York City at the start of the 1960s when women entrepreneurs were few and far between. When I visited her office in Manhattan at the impressionable age of 6, I was immediately mesmerized by the fact that she was the one in charge.

The name on the door of her business was Sue Carroll Personnel. Who was Sue Carroll? She was. She felt her surname, Ladenheim, might cause undue prejudice, so she changed it for the business. When Aunt Carol eventually got her own apartment near Lincoln Center, there were two names associated with her apartment: Carol Ladenheim and Sue Carroll. I always wondered if a strange woman might walk in the door one day and claim she was Sue Carroll.

Carol Landenheim in her Manhattan office, c. 1970

As I grew up, I often worked in her midtown office. At first, I handled clerical tasks. Then I upgraded to answering the phone and filing. But as I entered my teenage years, I grew to dislike the work I was given, endlessly filing little cards into grey or beige legal-size filing cabinets. I also didn't like the type of business she ran, filling medical assistant and nursing positions in doctors' offices or medical facilities. It was boring. However, she was still in charge and I was very attracted to that. I wanted to be in the workforce, earning my own income, not be a mom who stayed home caring for children.

We didn't have a lot of money growing up and there was nothing extra to go around. I grew up in a lower-middle-class area of the Bronx in a two-bedroom apartment. My mother was a homemaker, and my dad was a pattern cutter in New York's garment district. Money was a struggle for us, but my parents knew how to manage on a limited income. Whenever I asked my dad for extra money—as most teenagers do—he would shrug, pull out his pocket lining, and show me that all he had was a subway token.

To have my own money, I had to earn it and not be beholden to anyone. This was the early 1970s when women were just starting to flex their business muscles. In my family, women had two choices: either get married and eventually have children, or work for a living and probably never get married or have children. Aunt Carol was our family's example of option number two. She was the only one of her four sisters and one brother who didn't marry or have children. If I wanted to be in charge, like Aunt Carol, I figured having children was not going to be the main priority for me. In the end, that turned out to be a major decision, but not a very big sacrifice for me.

Most of the decisions I have made in my life center around this phrase: What's the worst that could happen? If I think really hard, I can come up with a laundry list of things that could go wrong in any situation. But I have the type of personality that allows me to plunge right in and take that leap off the cliff. If it doesn't work out, then I'll gather myself up and move on. In many instances, I've had to do just that.

Momentary distractions

Along with my desire to be an entrepreneur, I loved the idea that I could also be a performer one day. Where did that come from? Again, I point back to Aunt Carol.

My older brother was diagnosed with Leukemia when he was 8 years old. He was hospitalized much of the last couple of years of his life. During his long hospital stays, my mother's family members looked after my younger sister and me; mostly the job fell to our maternal grandmother. At the time, Aunt Carol lived with her parents while she was getting her business off the ground. She would go to her office, while my sister and I spent the day with Nana. We lived in the Jamaica section of Queens, very close to my grandparents, so it was easy for my parents to drop us off and pick us up.

When Aunt Carol returned home from work, she would pour herself a glass of scotch, settle down to relax, and ask her nieces to put on a show. The floor lamp would go on, my sister and I would collaborate on what we were going to do—sing, dance, act out a skit—and our audience of one cheered. I reveled in it. I'm not sure my sister loved it as much as I did, but she was a great sport. I was 6 or 7, and she was 5 years old.

I loved those performances and the attention we got. Shortly after my brother passed away, my family moved to the Bronx—which seemed far from Queens—where we attended the public elementary and middle schools.

During my middle school years, my love of performing continued. I earned high marks in class and was put into an accelerated academic program, skipping the eighth grade. When the time came to attend high school, I had the choice of attending either the local public high school or trying out for one of many specialty schools. The family thought I should apply to the school that specialized in math and science. I wanted to apply to the one specializing in performing arts. I applied to both. As it turned out, neither school accepted me, so I was off to the local high school where my grades quickly deteriorated.

It was the late 1960s, and the school I attended, Evander Childs, had built up a poor reputation over the years. It was a historic high school started by a well-known New York educator in a middle-class area of the Bronx in 1919. But by the time I started there, it had gained renown for being a rough school with lots of drug activities, interracial discord, and basic unrest. I did not do well in that environment. A combination of raging hormones, insecurity, teenage angst, and fear of going to school, made this an extremely unhappy time in my life. I went from an ordinary, fairly decent child to a rebellious, angry teenager. I barely made it through those years. Soon enough, I went off to the local city college, where I studied for two semesters, then quit.

I knew that if I wasn't going to attend school, I had to get a job. I didn't want to work for Aunt Carol anymore. I had various jobs until I landed a position working for an editor in the college textbook division at McGraw-Hill Book Company in Manhattan. Once my career was off and running, my parents breathed a sigh of relief.

McGraw-Hill had a tuition reimbursement program, and I took advantage of it. I completed three years at Fordham University in the Bronx while working full-time. As my studies advanced, opportunities opened up and I began to build a decent resume in the publishing industry. I stayed in professsional and textbook publishing, in and around the metro-New York area, for the next several years.

I moved to Atlanta in 1981 with my fiancé, Bob Kilgannon. He was given an opportunity to help launch a branch office of Bank of America. I was thrilled to go, and even then, I thought if it didn't work out, I would come home to New York and start again.

The professional and textbook publishing business was non-existent in Atlanta, so I worked a variety of temporary jobs to keep busy. One of the temp jobs I had was selling a test product called Bubble Yum, a chewing gum product packaged to resemble chewing tobacco. My job was to drive around a section of Atlanta selling to small grocery and convenience stores. This was quite an awakening for a young woman from New York, but it helped me learn how to navigate through my new hometown.

Once I learned my way around Atlanta, I concentrated on finding a full-time job where I could put the skills I learned in the publishing industry to use. Ideally, I wanted a position doing marketing and promotions. Off I went to find it.

MY CAREER ADVENTURES CONTINUE

2 |

■ ■ ■ ■ ■

"If you obey all the rules, you miss all the fun."
Katherine Hepburn

■ ■ ■ ■ ■

When I worked in New York City for major book publishers, people in sales positions were well regarded. Despite having had several jobs in these companies—editorial assistant, copywriter, advertising coordinator, and advertising manager—I never managed to make it into sales. If I wanted to continue in publishing, I knew I had to change my career direction from marketing to selling. This was definitely the trajectory needed to advance. My move to Atlanta waylaid those plans.

I knew that book publishing was a limited industry in the Atlanta market, so my chance of finding a decent gig in that field was slim to none. After weeks of searching for the perfect position, I finally landed that long-coveted job selling printing and mailing services.

In my previous jobs, I was often responsible for direct mail campaigns. This new opportunity required knowledge of direct mail marketing, so when the job was offered, I immediately jumped on the opportunity. Again, I repeated my mantra, "What's the worst that could happen? If it doesn't work out, then I will be off to find something else."

In the long run, that job became one of the stepping stones I needed to further my career. I was new to the city, and this job afforded me the opportunity to meet people I never would have met sitting in a cubicle. I didn't realize it at the time, but selling began to open doors to my future.

Taking risks

Taking risks when you are 27 is not too dangerous. At that age, you can bounce back if your decision backfires. The whole point of taking risks, in my opinion, was to get what I wanted, or at least to get closer to my goal. This meant I had to know what I wanted. Even in my twenties, there was always a motive for the chances I took. Taking the leap into a sales job didn't seem risky because I knew it would help in my career journey.

That position allowed me to peek into industries I knew nothing about: manufacturing, business services, financial institutions, retail, and various creative sectors. This job led me to the first ad agency I ever saw, and I was smitten. When I first stepped inside, it appealed to my visual sensibilities. It appeared glamorous, exciting, and different. I knew in that instant that I wanted to be part of it. Did I know this would lead me to my own advertising agency? Honestly, no. But it did confirm that I wanted to be in a creative business.

Almost every ad agency hums with energy. They are rarely sterile. No matter where the agency is located—whether in a concrete or steel business tower or in a converted warehouse—there is a sense of color, vibrancy, sight, sound, and motion often lacking in the typical corporate setting. I was determined to get into that environment, but I didn't know how. So I started asking. I knew it could be risky to jump into an entirely foreign workplace with little to no experience, but I was willing to give it a try; I wanted it that much.

One of my clients at the time ran the direct marketing division for a large, global advertising agency. As we were concluding a meeting, I came out and asked him, "Bart, how do I get a job in an advertising agency like this?"

He looked surprised and said, "Rena, you know more than many about the discipline of direct mail marketing. Why not write a letter to all the ad agency presidents in town and tell them you'd be happy to help them start a direct marketing unit."

I stared at him for what seemed like 10 minutes (probably more like 10 seconds) before I finally said, "That's it?"

"Yes," he said. "Most of the agencies are trying to figure out how to get a group started. I believe you can help. Just research who you need to send letters to, and do it."

"Okay," I said. "I'll give it a try."

Over the next couple of weeks, I researched the agencies and whom I needed to contact. I also included trend information as reported in the trade press about the urgent need for clients to add direct mail to their arsenal of marketing communications strategies. Nothing creates a sense of urgency in an agency faster than being the first to add a new service. Offering this in-house service would make them more relevant and could mean account wins and revenue growth.

I sent letters to the seven largest ad agencies and received a response from three. They wanted to talk about the potential this new service had for their firm. Each meeting went well, but there were no job offers. One agency was more intrigued than the others, but could not make it work at that time. I was very disappointed.

Meanwhile, as part of building my ad agency client base, I called on another firm that specialized in direct marketing. My contact was a print production manager, and I took the initiative to ask her the same question: "What do you suggest I do to try to move into the agency business?"

"Although you have direct marketing experience, you don't have an ad agency background," she said. "You would have to start at the bottom and work your way up."

"What type of job would that be?" I asked.

"If it's not the front desk, it would be any type of coordinator job."

"Do you know of any open jobs?" I ventured.

"No, but I'll let you know if I do," she said. Off I went. At least I'd planted a seed.

In hindsight, I realize I took a big risk asking this woman about a job. After all, I was at her office representing a vendor. I rationalized my actions with the sheer fact that I was curious about the advertising business. Besides that, I asked myself, "What's the worst that could happen?" Thankfully, it all worked out; at least, I thought so at the time. I'm not so sure I could pull off that kind of chutzpah today!

■ ■ ■ ■ ■

"I take risks all the time. I am always amazed at the
new things that will work for the business when I am
willing to give them a try."
Mitzi Moore, President, Sundial Plumbing

■ ■ ■ ■ ■

The seed I planted sprouted. A couple of weeks later, she phoned me and asked if I wanted to interview for a position in her agency as a traffic coordinator. Despite the fact that she knew I had no previous ad agency experience, she felt I could be a quick learner. A month later, I landed a job in an advertising agency.

I worked in that ad agency for one year before I was let go because of the loss of an account. I was devastated. This had never happened to me. However, I was not laid off due to performance issues; it was a financial decision. I didn't know what that meant at the time. Later, I learned that when an agency suffers an account loss, staff reductions almost always follow. The financial margins in the ad agency business are so thin, they do not allow for holding onto employees, hoping the agency will win another account. So I became a casualty.

THE LESSON: Don't sit on the sidelines waiting. Take a risk and make it happen for yourself. Was I this self-aware at age 27? No, but my boldness was instinctual. I knew what I wanted and went for it.

Despite the dismissal, I was grateful for the opportunity this firm gave me. I was quickly promoted to an account executive position after a short stint as the traffic coordinator. I learned how the business worked and found which of my skills were best suited for this industry. Now, I had the experience to move on and find another ad agency job.

One of my first steps was to reconnect with the firm that almost made the direct marketing position work for me the previous year. Why did I do that? Why not? What was the worst that could happen? It seemed an easier way to go than to start blindly looking for a job. I sent another letter, explaining that during the past year, I had increased my experience by working for the leading direct marketing agency and was now available to re-open the discussion we started previously.

This agency appointed a senior executive to pick up the discussion with me. As it turned out, the deal they wanted to make with me held a certain amount of risk. It was not a permanent position. The proposal was to create an independent contractor position as a specialist in direct marketing and test the idea with their current clients and prospects. This way, they would minimize their risk if none of their clients or prospects were interested in this new service offering. I agreed. After all, what's the worst that could happen? Nothing I couldn't survive.

THE LESSON: When you're riding high on a success, there is little that can stop you from wanting more. Go with that. Never fear taking risks.

I worked as an independent contractor for this large, nationally known ad agency and gained traction with its clients and prospects. I worked very hard to prove myself and became adept at promoting the benefits of direct mail as part of an overall marketing program. After nine months, they offered me a full-time, permanent position as vice president of a newly formed direct marketing division.

Steady training wheels

The appeal of calling my own shots and being in charge of the show, like my Aunt Carol, grew ever stronger as my career progressed. I was very successful with my division in the ad agency, and suddenly I was in charge of a growing staff. As I added business, there was a need to bring in a team to service the accounts. It was apparent that I had the skill to be effective, in part by managing a full staff of account managers and never getting too far removed from my clients' marketing goals. I began to understand the draw of being the boss, calling the shots, making difficult decisions, and learning how to responsibly run my portion of the business.

I knew I had to learn the inner workings of the business, how the financials worked and the implications when they didn't. I often sought the council of the CFO following management meetings when he pointed out how well my group was doing in comparison to others in the agency. I wanted to know more, and he started me on the road to learning how ad agency finances work. Some of it stuck, some of it didn't. But one thing I learned was how important it is to pay attention to the numbers.

At the time, all I knew was the importance of achieving revenue goals. I had no idea how the expense side of the equation worked. I wanted to know so I would continue to be a profit contributor rather than an expense drain. By meeting weekly with the CFO, I learned how my revenues and related expenses compared and contributed to the rest of the company's numbers. This was my first lesson in grasping the revenue versus expense equation. It also helped me understand how well other departments were performing compared to mine. I soon found out that my team was outperforming the others. Despite the success of my small group, the agency was not doing well. With consideration to the agency's overall weakening financial performance, a decision was made by our holding company out of New York to merge our agency into a sister firm from Dallas, Texas.

The HR people came in to evaluate everyone, and I quickly learned that there were going to be some changes. For the first time in a long time, I felt threatened. I had a great relationship with my clients, my staff, and my superiors. I was even hitting and exceeding my projections. I realized that, despite these positive factors, my future was not in my hands. Looking for another job did not occur to me. At that moment, I decided to launch my own business. I thought, "What's the worst that could happen if owning my own business doesn't work out? I'll just go out and get another job." Sound familiar?

The Kilgannon Group

In 1988, I decided to start an advertising agency in Atlanta. I knew I needed a client or two if I wanted to launch a real company. Too many times, executives leave companies and hope to start a successful business without customers. I was determined to open my ad agency with a business plan, which included starting with a customer base. That meant getting a client *before* I officially opened the door. I had the perfect client in mind, and I had the perfect pitch to explain why and how I could do it better for them.

One hitch was that I had signed a non-compete clause with the ad agency I'd just left. Technically, I could not start a company that would compete with the agency, or I could be taken to court and open myself up to a lawsuit. But the stars were aligned for me due to several factors that struck down the non-compete. It turned out that my lead client was so specific about ensuring my involvement that they wrote me into their contract. Essentially, the contract noted that if I no longer worked on their account, they had the right to cancel. Once I left the company, the clause went into effect immediately.

I approached this client and informed them of my decision to start my own firm. I also reminded them about the contract clause that included me. It was at this point that the client suggested I meet with the CEO of the company to discuss my proposal to start my own agency and bring them on as my first client. This was a big risk. I was scared out of my mind. What if the CEO didn't like my proposal? I needed to be prepared to make the case as to why working with me would benefit them.

I prepared a presentation that enumerated the reasons they should move their account to my newly formed agency, including the financial benefits. I also proposed we try the relationship for a period of time. If they didn't feel they were getting any benefit, I would personally help them find another firm.

■ ■ ■ ■ ■

"I'm always thinking and planning ahead, so I can minimize risk. But I am not afraid of it. The consequences are about not taking the risks at all."
A. Lizz Patrick, Founder, Patrick Law Group

■ ■ ■ ■ ■

As confident as I was in myself, I had some reservations. What if they said "no"? What would I do? Start the agency anyway? I was so convinced my argument to win the business was strong—including having the endorsement of a key executive—that even though I was worried, I knew my case was compelling. In essence, this was an all or nothing gamble, and I had to take the risk to make my dream of running my own company happen.

I presented my case to the CEO. He listened, and asked me if they would be my only client. Gulp.

"Yes, for now," I said. There was a long, painful pause.

His reply was firm: "I don't want the responsibility of being your only client. What if something happens and we leave? I don't want to be responsible for putting you out of business."

I didn't think of this when I was putting my plan together. I could feel my face flush and my blood pressure go up. I probably turned a shade of purple. I didn't respond right away. When I was able to collect myself, I asked him if he would give me a couple of months to find additional clients. I would report back to him when I gained another client or two in order to take any burden off of his shoulders. He agreed with that proposal. By the time I left the meeting, I was spent. What did I promise? How was I going to meet this obligation? I had no plan for this scenario. This time, I believed I had walked right into the worst thing that could happen: my plan could backfire.

I had to figure out how to find new clients. Any prospect I approached would want to know what I had done for other companies. They would want me to prove my value. I had a track record with the ad agency I had just left, but none with my new firm. Despite the fact that I had earned a reputation for my knowledge of direct marketing, I was running a brand new, unproven organization. I needed to gain momentum and craft messaging for my new firm. I had one client (at least at the time). It was important to relay the information about my company to other business professionals I knew, so they could refer me, or better yet, hire me to do work for them.

The threat of failure caused me to put all of my knowledge and resources into action. I recalled a conversation with a friend of mine who worked for a Fortune 500 company. "I'm working with someone in our licensing division who might need some help," she said. "Why don't I introduce you?" That was all I needed: the introduction and endorsement of a strong influencer. The Kilgannon Group got the assignment, and better yet, this impressive company's name landed on my client list.

I examined my competitive set and realized that I didn't have much direct competition locally. I was a specialist in direct marketing, and many of the local ad agencies did not offer this service. I also set up my company differently than the typical ad agency. I purposefully did not have a full-service firm. I staffed the firm with account managers only, and outsourced all of my creative work to freelancers. This kept our overhead low and saved clients money. In addition, it opened the door to working with other agencies, because my agency posed little or no threat. As we collaborated on projects, they kept the creative work while I worked on the planning and selling. Within a few months, my fledgling company had three clients, a couple of them ad agencies. Whew! I was off and running.

In the beginning, I made it work, despite operating with a slightly different business model. I was able to complete assignments on time and on budget while building my reputation as a subject matter expert.

I had one large client and a couple of small, project-based clients. I hired two staff members to run the day-to-day account activities. It was my responsibility to continue to grow the business and to run the administrative side. Someone had to pay the bills, issue client invoices, and keep track of expenses. This became my weekend job. In less time than I thought, I was my own boss, running a successful ad agency—on a wing and a prayer, but it was running! The risks I took paid off. Finally, I had stepped into Aunt Carol's shoes, and it felt great.

THE LIFE
OF AN
3 | ENTREPRENEUR

■ ■ ■ ■ ■

"Entrepreneurs are different."
James V. Koch, *Born, Not Made: The Entrepreneurial Personality*

■ ■ ■ ■ ■

There is a lot of pride associated with being an entrepreneur. In the early days of my business, people asked me what I did, and I told them I owned and ran an advertising agency. Often, that evoked a reaction of wide-eyed surprise—even though it was momentary—and the response was usually, "Wow! That's great. Who are some of your clients?" Or "How big is your company?" At first, I was reluctant to tell anyone who my clients were or how many employees I had. My clients were in specialized categories, in vertical businesses, and were not brands anyone would recognize. There was something about being so small at the start that held me back. I didn't think I would be taken seriously. I didn't want people to think that I was just dabbling in between jobs.

A couple of years went by, and there seemed to be a grudging respect from my peers that I was still around running my own business. I loved those early days. The Kilgannon Group turned into a 24/7 endeavor. I ran it during the week and came into the office on Saturday and Sunday to do administrative tasks: paying the bills, filing, organizing for the upcoming week, and so on. The trials and tribulations of work were always on my mind. Problems, challenges, and ideas often woke me up at three o'clock in the morning. But these were distinctly mine. I was not worrying about office politics or how I could get promoted or what my next performance review would look like.

Rena Kilgannon in her Atlanta office, 1996

As I progressed, I discovered traits about myself—and the people around me—that surprised, delighted, and horrified me. Although I would have liked to think I was good at everything when it came to running the business, I was not. This realization came as I grew the business and added more employees. When there were five of us, everyone knew what was going on. As the staff grew, it was hard to keep pace. I learned that once the business scaled up, the interoffice dynamics changed. We were forming our own personality, and it was happening despite me.

Born or made?

The traits, skills, and personality attributes of entrepreneurs always interested me. Was I truly entrepreneurial, or did I just think I was? At the end of the day, the answer is yes, I am a true entrepreneur, but in my discovery of what makes someone an entrepreneur, I learned that there is a special combination of risk, daring, and nerve required before someone can truly claim that moniker.

Are entrepreneurs born or made? While interviewing women entrepreneurs for this book, I learned the answer: both. I placed these women (and other entrepreneurs) into three categories: accidental, native, and family.

The term "accidental entrepreneur" has been popularized by many writers, among them Susan Urquhart-Brown, who wrote the book *The Accidental Entrepreneur: 50 Things I Wish Someone Had Told Me About Starting a Business*. Then there are bloggers like Kerry McQuaide, and reporters, like Sarah Needleman of *The Wall Street Journal*. Although each has a different take on the topic, I borrow this phrase and thank them for the use of the term. One trait they each cite is that accidental entrepreneurs never had being a small business owner in their master plan.

■ ■ ■ ■ ■

"I had dinner with a friend who told me my problem was that I would always stand out in a firm like this because I have the skills and the thinking of an entrepreneur. I should consider starting my own firm and running the practice of law for my clients in the way I believed was best."
A. Lizz Patrick, Founder, Patrick Law Group

■ ■ ■ ■ ■

Then there are the "native entrepreneurs." My use of the term refers to people who always dreamed of owning and running a small business. Entrepreneurship comes instinctively to them. I use the term "native" the way the millennial generation is often referred to as digital natives. It just comes naturally.

Lastly, there are family entrepreneurs. In this case, entrepreneurship might be a generational next step for many—whether they like it or not—or a role they were lucky to be born into. Often, those in family enterprises are expected to work in the business. At the very least, they have entrepreneurship as a secure career option.

Many look at starting and running a business as brave. Those of us who have accomplished this—whether accidentally or purposefully—don't think of this trait as applicable to us. We look at running a business as something we have to try. It's uncomfortable, and often a source of regret, not to feed the monster inside that begs to create something, grow it into a successful venture, call our own shots, and contribute to the economy by hiring others. I believe most accidental and native entrepreneurs think, "If this doesn't work, something else will."

As my friend Ellen Dracos Lemming said during our interview, "No one is going to die. If my business goes under, I'll reinvent myself." It's an outlook most of us share.

In September 2013, *Entrepreneur* magazine addressed the mystery of the entrepreneur in "Are Entrepreneurs Born or Made?" by Jason Daley. Academics, and those who give this a lot of thought, study us as if we are some sort of rare bird. There are now schools focused on entrepreneurship, and many books written about this topic. I'm fascinated by all of this.

Daley's article describes the multiple studies conducted over the past five years that indicate there may be an "entrepreneur gene" or at least that people with certain genetic characteristics and personality traits are more likely than others to be successful entrepreneurs.

James V. Koch of Old Dominion University in Norfolk, Virginia, co-authored a book with James L. Fisher in 2008 called *Born, Not Made: The Entrepreneurial Personality*. This book argues that many entrepreneurs are simply wired that way, giving them a natural advantage in the business world. This parallels with my reference to "native entrepreneurs."

The authors' findings were very familiar to my own behavior, as well as to that of many entrepreneurs I know. Here are some interesting points:

- Some personalities are much more favorable for entrepreneurship. If you want to know who's more likely to be an entrepreneur, don't go to a business school and see who has taken entrepreneurship courses. Look at someone's personality and ability to bear risks. "I'm not sure you can teach somebody to love to take risks. It seems hard-wired in the individual," the authors note in the article.

- When asked if entrepreneurship comes from an interaction of heredity and the environment, the authors say, "Significant portions of personality traits critical to entrepreneurs, like the willingness to take risks and the ability to tolerate ambiguity and uncertainty, are heritable." Thanks, Aunt Carol!

- When asked about the specific characteristics of an entrepreneur, the authors suggest that entrepreneurs have a personality that is mercurial. They have highs that are really high and lows that are really low. There is good evidence that they have strong self-confidence, but also tend to be overly optimistic. They rely on their own intuition.

- A very large proportion of entrepreneurs fail. They tend not to be as devoted to consensus decision-making. They violate status quo more often. Many don't accept defeat or losses gracefully. They are energetic, and a high percentage of them tend to be loners and work long hours. While all these things appear in other segments of the population, they appear more commonly among entrepreneurs.

I agree with the authors on many of the statements they make in their book and what they found in these studies. What is not specified is where women entrepreneurs differ from men.

In June 2012, *Forbes* published "Seven Traits of Incredibly Successful Entrepreneurs," written by Eric Wagner. He identifies a number of traits with which I am in complete agreement: abounding curiosity, loving risk, and taking action. He mentions other points, such as having clarity of vision and leadership acumen.

Being relentlessly curious is one trait mentioned in Wagner's article that helped me in business. I wanted to know more about my clients' businesses, what made them tick, how I could serve them better. I was curious about the inner workings of my industry. I participated in many national ad agency events, so I could learn how other agencies operated. Much of what I learned over the years helped me be a more effective businessperson. For me, knowledge is power, and I always wanted to know more.

■ ■ ■ ■ ■

"There are three attributes I have that helped me:
1) I have intense engagement and focus for the
business; 2) I am a student of the business and I
accessed a lot of outside advisors; and 3) I had really
big doses of courage. I was willing to fail."
Mitzi Moore, President, Sundial Plumbing

■ ■ ■ ■ ■

Another article, written for the tech industry, was posted on IncomeDiary.com. This one, titled "6 Traits All Entrepreneurs Secretly Have in Common," by Nick Scheidies, resonated most with me, particularly in my experience with entrepreneurs, as we are truly naïve and masters of nothing. According to Scheidies:

- Entrepreneurs are down to earth.
- Entrepreneurs are naïve.
- Entrepreneurs are lucky.
- Entrepreneurs are masters of nothing.
- Entrepreneurs are compassionate.
- Entrepreneurs are different.

At the end of the day, innocence and hopefulness encourage entrepreneurs to move forward, whereas the more thoughtful among us pause and ponder the outcomes. Traditionally, entrepreneurs skip that step.

Entrepreneur magazine, in 2007, published an article by James Stephenson listing the 25 characteristics of successful home-based entrepreneurs. Despite the title, the inventory reads more like a to-do list than a litany of traits that generate success:

1. Do what you enjoy.
2. Take what you do seriously.
3. Plan everything.
4. Manage money wisely.
5. Ask for the sale.
6. Remember, it's all about the customer.
7. Become a shameless self-promoter.
8. Project a positive business image.
9. Get to know your customers.
10. Level the playing field with technology.
11. Build a top-notch business team.
12. Become known as an expert.
13. Create a competitive advantage.
14. Invest in yourself.
15. Be accessible.
16. Build a rock-solid reputation.
17. Sell benefits.
18. Get involved.
19. Grab attention.
20. Master the art of negotiation.
21. Design your workspace for success.
22. Get and stay organized.
23. Take time off.
24. Limit the number of hats you wear.
25. Follow-up constantly.

For those who lack the skill—or the nerve—to handle the items on this list, I suggest seeking the right counsel. I was never good at becoming a "shameless self-promoter," although I wished I had been.

Becoming any kind of entrepreneur requires more than a task list. It also requires capital. There are various ways to secure that capital: venture capital, private equity investors, personal savings, business partners, and so on. Some of the items on the previous list require money. Starting a new business is often costly. Where the money comes from requires serious thought.

The cushion

During my conversations with women entrepreneurs, I found a common theme. As it turns out, many of them might not have been able to pursue their entrepreneurial goals if not for what I call "the cushion." For transparency purposes, let me say that I found myself among the "cushion set," so I pass no judgment.

What is the cushion? The cushion is financial in nature. Plainly, it is having the financial flexibility—often provided by a personal partner—to pursue entrepreneurial goals. This could be a spouse or life partner, parent, close friend, or someone else who provides the entrepreneur with financial security during the start-up period. I am not talking about business incubators or venture capital investors. I am also not referring to those who have saved enough money to launch a business. Sometimes, the entrepreneur has saved some money but needs more. I am referring to someone close to the entrepreneur who provides financial assistance either with day-to-day living expenses or as seed money for the new business venture. There are personal consequences with this, as there is an emotional connection not found when an outside investor is involved.

I did it.

■ ■ ■ ■ ■

"I could work four hours and stay home with my
babies. I could take the risk because my husband was
earning six figures at the time."
Stacy Williams, President, Prominent Placement, Inc.

■ ■ ■ ■ ■

I didn't want to work out of the house when I started my business, primarily because the client who started with me was from Orlando, Florida, and liked to travel to Atlanta for business meetings. At the time, I also thought it would legitimize my company if I had a physical location from which to operate. This was prior to the inexpensive-personal-computing, mobile-business, easy-access-to-technology days that rapidly evolved to create a boon for entrepreneurs. Working from anywhere wasn't as easy as it is today.

I had the cushion. My husband, Bob, held an executive position with a large international bank, and he earned enough to keep us going while I was in the start-up phase. At the time, I didn't have enough money saved, so I borrowed money from him. I needed office space, furniture, and a computer. I needed money for legal and other business services. Bob lent me the money. Was there an emotional price to pay? Yes. Did it interfere with our personal relationship and affect our marriage. On and off, yes, but we worked hard to overcome it.

■ ■ ■ ■ ■

"Starting my company was a risk. I was fortunate
to have a financial cushion through my marriage.
I probably wouldn't have tried it if I didn't have
the cushion."
Ellen Dracos Lemming, President, Dracos-Lemming, LLC

■ ■ ■ ■ ■

I often wonder if I could have done it without that cushion. During two different interviews for this book, a couple of my colleagues also mentioned that they were fortunate enough to have a cushion. In all of our cases, this was a great impetus to venture into the unknown of starting our businesses. Each cited an emotional consequence, which they overcame. We all agreed the cushion was distracting for a time, and it became one more thing to add to the pressure most new entrepreneurial ventures encounter.

It was important to me to repay Bob. Doing so would prove I was capable of debt repayment. I paid him back in year two and never borrowed money from our household again. I did have a line of credit (LOC) with my bank for a short period, but my CFO business partner insisted it was not necessary for a service business to ever depend on an LOC. After all, we were not in the manufacturing or retail business and didn't need capital to carry us over for a period of time. If we had a responsible billing and receivable policy, there would never be a need. Getting an LOC or borrowing money for the short term is necessary for some businesses; it just wasn't necessary for mine.

On the contrary, there are a lot of very successful entrepreneurs who had no cushion and made it work. Those are the business owners who I believe are the biggest heroes. To do it on your own—without any cushion as I've described—is very admirable.

DO YOU
NEED A
4 | BUSINESS PLAN?

■ ■ ■ ■ ■

"It takes as much energy to wish as it does to plan."
Eleanor Roosevelt

■ ■ ■ ■ ■

When many people start their businesses, they sit down—
sometimes alone, sometimes with an advisor—and write a
business plan. It could outline a simple approach, or be an MBA-
style business plan with financial projections, analytics, and stats
that would make any banker or investor proud. This doesn't
mean you'll get any money, but it might be a good exercise.

I had a business plan of sorts when I started out, but once I
landed my first account, I never looked at it again. It was five
pages long, and did not include financial projections. I wouldn't
classify it as a business plan today.

After being in business for several years, my partner asked
me annually to project how many clients, employees, and revenue dollars I hoped to gain over the next five years. I did so,
but my projections were short descriptions that looked like this:

2002 – 5 clients, 15 employees, $200K gross income
2003 – 7 clients, 22 employees, $250K gross income

I never described some of the basic necessities of a plan. How did I intend to find and add these new clients? What were the details behind these somewhat obscure numbers I was projecting? Not exactly a plan. However, he worked from these vague projections to fill in the financial blanks.

■ ■ ■ ■ ■

"I live by the three-month rule. I am constantly looking down the road, three months out, six months out. I make lists and I keep journals. I try to get ahead of myself all the time. Mostly, so I can prepare and plan for what might be next."
A. Lizz Patrick, Founder, Patrick Law Group

■ ■ ■ ■ ■

When I started, there was a dearth of ad agencies that specialized in direct marketing, so I knew instinctively that there was a target audience. My naïvety lay in proving it. I never spoke to clients about the need for an agency like mine, nor did I look at industry projections. Since I ventured out with one client already in hand, I didn't think this was necessary. However, I now know it's a good idea to record business goals and review them regularly. These goals are a reminder that there are objectives to meet.

I struggled with reviewing my goals, and often went on a quest with this consultant or that executive coach to help me. At the end of the day, I had to learn the discipline and importance of building a plan and sticking with it, as long as it was relevant for my company.

When you own your business and don't have investors, no one holds you accountable for your goals. Business planning keeps an entrepreneur accountable. The plan for my company became reliant on our annual revenue performance. In the fourth quarter of each year, we reviewed how we did and forecasted what the next year would look like. By then, many of our clients had been through their budget planning process, so we knew what they had designated for their marketing program. Sometimes their budgets went up, and sometime they stayed the same. We were able to project our revenue based on the clients' budgets, but we also had to forecast additional projects and revenue. Could we get more from existing clients, or would our revenue growth depend on bringing in new business?

These were goals we had to try to achieve at the start of each new year. But who was holding us accountable? As it turned out, one of our most important assets—our employees— looked to us to help them define their role in achieving the agency's goals. The performance and delivery of these goals for the business involved them, and we needed to be clear about how we expected our team to perform.

Performance and accountability

I knew how important it was for every stakeholder in the company to succeed. As much as I hated goal setting, I found that others were looking for how they could participate in helping the agency grow. One opportunity to recognize how well employees were contributing to the agency was during their annual performance reviews.

I didn't like doing performance reviews for employees. I loathed the thought of the conversation about whether or not they achieved their goals over the past year. However, I have been told that employees like knowing where they stand. They need feedback as to whether they are on the right track. I failed at this miserably. After all, who was there to ensure that I was getting feedback on my own performance?

Employees had to remind me to conduct their performance

reviews. They wanted to know my point of view as to whether or not they were meeting their goals. If they were doing well, would they get a raise or promotion? Just because these reviews didn't work for me, didn't mean they weren't important to others. But to me, this was a backward view of whether employees did their job over a defined period of time. The entire process seemed artificial to me.

When I had a smaller employee base, I promised quarterly bonuses. It was at these sessions that I reviewed their work over the past few months, and I often handed them a check at the end of the conversation. The process took all of 10 minutes, and at the end they walked away with a reward. It was a win-win for both sides. As we added more employees, this process reverted to the more traditional annual performance review format, which I hated.

Over time, I learned to manage the review and accountability of our staff. I accepted these responsibilities as a necessary function of being a successful entrepreneur. Once I got through the reviews, I reasoned, I could focus my attention on things I valued much more.

Executive coach—finally, someone to hold me accountable

No one ever really holds entrepreneurs accountable for their performance in leading a business. Continuous improvement in meeting and exceeding business goals is out in the open for all to see. But for leadership performance, not so much.

At a conference attended by other independent advertising agencies from around the country, there was a presentation given by an executive coach. I don't remember much about the presentation itself, but the information packet included an offer for a free one-hour session. Since I loved to discuss the challenges of our business with complete strangers, I signed up.

That decision led to a very rewarding, multi-year relationship with an executive coach. We spoke once a month for 90-minute sessions. In our first session, she helped me identify the issues that were holding me back. She proposed a program designed to help me with areas I needed to improve and laid out how she would provide the guidance I needed. This coach was also a former executive in the advertising industry, and it was helpful that I didn't have to explain how an advertising agency works. She was familiar with the nuances of our business, and that eliminated any learning curve. However, executive coaches are often trained to focus on the whole person and her or his business interactions. It's not necessary or important that executive coaches are conversant in any particular industry. They just need to know the basics of business dynamics.

I was now accountable to an outside, non-biased professional. Her program helped me confront several issues that were keeping me from achieving greater success. Some of the issues involved my lack of confidence, interpersonal business relationships that were counterproductive, and my avoidance of completing routine tasks.

Executive coaching was a positive experience. I strived to change my behaviors when I encountered challenging situations. I worked on a more organized business development process. Being accountable to her forced me to pay more attention to the tasks I was avoiding. All of this helped to build my confidence.

Unfortunately, when the recession hit, I had to give up the coaching due to budget cuts. Periodically though, I called her for a session, and although that arrangement wasn't ideal, her advice reminded me of the strategies I needed to implement: identify and celebrate my accomplishments, identify what I did not accomplish, and record lessons learned along the way.

In an article titled "How to Pick an Executive Coach," published in *Psychology Today,* valid points were cited that are important when considering this option:

- **It helps to know why you need an executive coach.** Coaching is an expensive endeavor, so be sure your coach can help with specific challenges you have. Talk to other entrepreneurs who have worked with executive coaches to learn what they got out of it.

- **Executive coaches are not consultants.** The only resemblance is they are an "outside" advisor and not on your staff. They bill you and, from my experience, expect payment within 10 days.

- **Negotiate a practice session.** You want to make sure there is a connection, so a session for free or at a substantially reduced cost is a good way to try them on. If it works out, you've probably found the right person. Don't forget good chemistry; it helps enormously if you like each other.

If you have found your ideal coach, set objectives and timelines for deliverables. This keeps you and the coach accountable.

I believed there was a connection between the growth of the company and the help I got from an executive coach. Can I quantify it? No, but emotionally I felt someone at a professional level had my back.

Peer-to-peer "therapy" groups

Entrepreneurs can benefit greatly from resources that provide support, guidance, and the opportunity to build professional relationships. I never hesitated to seek the counsel of others, and I found that it helped me—and the business—grow.

I love brainstorming with others who have the same issues I do. So I was honored when my trade association recommended me to participate in a forum of agencies from around the country. The trade association grouped agencies of similar sizes from different markets, and they met twice per year. Each group was comprised of one agency representing a geographic region, to avoid competitive conflicts. The session included a discussion of "burning issues," during which members of the group discussed challenges they faced in their firms. I referred to this as group therapy. We also had a featured speaker or a visit to a large local agency.

I was part of a forum for more than 10 years. I loved each meeting—not only for the camaraderie, but also for the insights I gained. Great friendships were made, and even better, I learned practices I could implement at my agency. In addition, these meetings provided access to some of the best ad agencies in the country, many of which I wouldn't have connected with if not for my participation in these teams.

It is essential that entrepreneurs associate with like-minded peers in a facilitated forum, where they can speak openly about the business challenges they face. During these forums, everyone was very transparent, which allowed participants to confess sensitive issues that served as lessons for the other attendees. One of my colleagues confided that a long-time employee who had access to the company's funds had recently "cooked the books." Details of the theft were scary and caused us all to question those in our companies who handled our money. Another colleague wanted to fire a family member who was not performing. At times, it was cathartic to talk to others who often found themselves in similar circumstances.

Though immensely helpful, these frank conversations reminded us of how lonely entrepreneurship can be.

TAKE RESPONSIBILITY
5 | FOR DECISIONS

■ ■ ■ ■ ■

*"Every excuse I ever heard made perfect sense
to the person who made it."*
Dr. Daniel T. Drubin

■ ■ ■ ■ ■

There are two things I do not like in business or anywhere else: the blame game and making excuses. Failing to take responsibility for a decision or business problem is not a positive trait; I can spot the perpetrator a mile away. Similarly, when someone makes excuses, I can usually detect what is legitimate and what is not. I also know when I am about to make excuses, and I try to stop myself. The truth is always easier to deal with than a big, fat lie.

As a business owner, the buck stopped at my door. When a client was unhappy with the service we offered, there was no finger-pointing that was acceptable to me. Even if there was something or someone else who was directly responsible, I, as owner of the company, had to take the fall. That responsibility comes with having your name on the door.

Over the years, I had many employees who were directly responsible for mistakes. Many of them owned up to them; a few did not. When they blamed someone else or an event out of their control, I took note for future one-on-one discussions. If I was their direct supervisor, the issue was discussed right away or at performance review time. If one of my managers supervised the employee, I requested they include a discussion and a plan for subsequent action during the performance review.

One staff member constantly passed the buck. Nothing was ever this person's fault. There was always someone or a circumstance to point to if something went wrong. This was very frustrating for everyone. But this particular employee was not the only one who did this.

In one instance, we were planning a campaign to help a client develop a name for a new product. I had a seasoned staff that knew how to prepare for this, so off they went into a brainstorming session. When they emerged, they brought me their ideas. I was disappointed and explained why.

By this time in the company's growth, it was not necessary for me to approve work that went to the client. I had very competent managers and business partners who knew how to prepare work, present it, and provide rationale for it. However, in this case, they missed the mark—by a mile. Unfortunately, in this instance, I did not view the team's recommendations before they presented them to the client. As it turned out, some of the concepts were too edgy for this southern, conservative client.

After the team's presentation of our ideas, the client called to request a meeting with me—no staff involved. I knew what it was about right away: they were not happy with the work. I went to their office accompanied by my business partner to demonstrate that we knew how important this meeting was and that it necessitated the full engagement of the leadership of The Kilgannon Group.

During the meeting, the client brought up a litany of issues that had nothing to do with the campaign that the staff had recently presented. This was obviously an unhappy client who wanted the leadership of the agency to know they were displeased. I was embarrassed and angry. But for the client's benefit (and that of my staff), I accepted the responsibility for the failure. When I went back to the office, I told the staff this client was unhappy, and why, and what I wished to do about it.

I took responsibility for the day-to-day activity on the account for several weeks. I wanted to see—upfront and personal—what was going on that precipitated this client's reactions. From the most mundane tasks all the way through more complex aspects of running the account, I noticed challenges that could be viewed by the client as failures or incompetencies.

Despite my stepping in, I knew the client would soon cancel the contract. The problem was too far gone to expect a turnaround. But my staff knew how unhappy I was, and they rallied to do the best they could do under the circumstances. We all realized that the client was looking for reasons to let us go. They eventually sent us a letter canceling the contract and chose an advertising agency that specialized in their business sector. It was the right decision for them and a great lesson for me. Did I get too far away from my clients' accounts? Was this happening with other clients?

Taking responsibility for the mistakes of others is one of the hardest things to do as a business owner. It's easy to blame a wayward colleague. But if your name is on the door and your reputation is in others' hands, responsibility is a given; it's not a choice.

When things go wrong, both sides—whether the agency or the client and their respective employees—have a tendency to blame the other side or make excuses for their own shortcomings. Even if they take responsibility, there's an excuse hidden there somewhere. It is rare when complete and raw honesty emerges. But sometimes transparency helps the other party move on or improve.

Impulsive vs. compulsive: the risks

No one said that sound decisions use logic as a base. In fact, I have made many decisions on the fly that had no basis in reality. Such are the ways of entrepreneurs, particularly those of us in creative businesses; we are often dreamers. Early on, I had no road map to distinguish good decisions from ones that could be potentially damaging. Thankfully, as I grew into the business and learned not to react without considering all aspects of the issue, my logical thinking and reasoning improved.

However, ask anyone, and they will tell you that I am impulsive. Many of my advisors have attempted to teach me how to lessen the number of times I jump into commitments without considering the consequences. After all, what's the worst that could happen?

I believe there is a fine line between being impulsive and being compulsive. Impulsive people act without forethought. Some of the synonyms for impulsive are: impetuous, spontaneous, hasty, emotional, and reckless. Compulsive actions result from or relate to an irresistible urge, especially one that is against one's conscious wishes. Synonyms associated with compulsive include: irresistible, uncontrollable, compelling, urgent, and overwhelming.

I am a mix of both. For instance, I am a *compulsive* shopper. There are times when I make retail purchases that are irresistible, compelling, and urgent. There are very few women I know who don't have the periodic compulsive shopping trip. Sometimes I can overcome it, sometimes not.

I have occasionally made compulsive decisions in business. I usually did this when I felt my back was against the wall and I had no choice. Sometimes it had to do with hiring people—people I never should have hired, but because I was panicked, I went ahead and did it. Other times it had to do with reacting to a frustrated client.

Unfortunately, as a business owner, this compulsive behavior paid me back. In the case of one employee I should not have hired, it cost me in more ways than one. She turned out to be a high-maintenance individual who once asked that the overhead lights in the office be turned off because she had a headache. She quit unexpectedly, and erased all of her computer files, which included important client correspondence. Fortunately, we had a systematic back-up program, and we were able to retrieve many of the missing documents. But it cost money and employee time to rebuild the file. As another example, I chose the wrong vendor for a client project, only to be burned. Every time I acted compulsively, it cost me a lot of money.

When it comes to being *impulsive*, the causative factor is typically my feeling of being deprived of something. As I grew my company and networked with all the right people, I wanted material things that these important people had. If someone of prestige bought a $5,000 table at a charity event, I wanted to as well. Fortunately for me, there was someone of sound mind, as well as financial stewardship, to stop me. I recall telling Mike Reineck, the company CFO and my business partner, that while I was CEO of the company, he was CEO of the money. He had the right to overrule me when it came to making impulsive financial decisions.

How does being either impulsive or compulsive affect the company?

There can be both negative and positive consequences. Here are some of the lessons learned:

- **Think before acting.** I have implemented a new rule: TAKE A BREATH! Before taking action, say, "Let me think about it," or "I'll get back to you on that."

- **There will always be French toast.** One of my avocations is as a professional dieter. I am constantly trying to shed a few pounds. With this in mind, I can't always have the food I crave, like French toast. When I crave something, I remind myself that there will always be French toast; it's not going anywhere. If I take off a few pounds and want to reward myself, I can have French toast. Apply this thinking to anything rash you want to do for the business. Most of the time, the thing you are going to do impulsively, will likely be there tomorrow. You don't have to jump on it today.

- **Compulsion is dangerous.** When people act compulsively, it is indicative of a larger problem. Often, when compulsion hits, you're panicked for some reason. Many times I stopped whatever I was doing and stepped away for a while. Nothing positive comes out of fear.

- **Great entrepreneurs are impulsive.** It's going to happen. Embrace it. Entrepreneurs, by definition, are risk takers. Taking risks may require making decisions on the fly, which could be read as impulsive. But that is how an entrepreneur is built. It's in our DNA.

6 | ASK FOR WHAT YOU WANT

■ ■ ■ ■ ■

"Begin, be bold, and venture to be wise."
Horace

■ ■ ■ ■ ■

My dad was never afraid to ask for things if he wanted or needed them. He worked in the garment industry in New York City during a time when many jobs were going overseas. When he was laid off, he would not go to the union office and wait to be called for a job. Instead, he walked around the garment industry and knocked on doors to find out if anyone needed him. He usually ended up with a job because he wasn't afraid to ask. Deaf since birth and with no high school diploma, he was a remarkable man. He was a risk taker, who always made things happen.

For lots of people, asking for help is sometimes daunting. Whether the resistance comes from fear of rejection, fear of looking incompetent, or something else, the prospect of asking stops many people dead in their tracks. Oftentimes they think (or act as if) they've got it all figured out, when they really don't. So they play the game and fake it until they make it. But aid doesn't just appear out of the ether. I learned that early in life. If I don't know how to do something, I'll reach out to someone who knows more than I do.

My ability to ask is deeply rooted in my approach. Some might call it a system, but that sounds much too formal. Actually, it all goes back to that question: what's the worst that could happen?

Here are a few things to consider:

- What specifically do you need help with?

- Who is most capable of providing the assistance you need in a timely manner?

- Who do you need to call to get the ball rolling?

That's it. It's just that simple. I have learned to recognize when I need counsel and then ask whomever I believe to be the most competent person to help me.

Asking for things such as recognition, a particular job or board position, or something tangible, can be daunting. By the time I opened The Kilgannon Group, I had a great need for recognition amongst my own industry peer group: the owners and presidents of local ad agencies. I volunteered at the Ad Club, a non-profit group where many of them met on a regular basis. I thought I had to infiltrate this group by offering my time, so I stepped up and pitched in for events or helped out at luncheons.

Eventually, I asked to be put on the Ad Club board, and I was. Consequently, I became the board chair for two terms. In time, this helped me gain the recognition I sought, and satisfied my need to be acknowledged. But it was too "local" for me. I wanted something bigger.

There was a local board of governors of the national advertising association. As a member, I received an annual ballot to approve the slate of members who were on the council. They were all very important ad agency leaders, and I wanted to be one of them. I noticed that all the candidates were men. I heard there was once a woman on the council, but I'm convinced that was a rumor.

I was in New York at the trade association's home office, and I asked the representative in charge of our area what it would take to get on the local council. "Oh," he said, "you want to sit on the Atlanta board council? I'll make a call and suggest it." Right there, he picked up the phone and called the chair of the council and said, "Rena Kilgannon wants to sit on the council board. Any objections?" The reply was immediate. "No objection, sounds good. She's on." That simple.

That simple? In this case, yes. In other cases, not so much. All I thought about was bracing myself for rejection. It didn't come. I realized that if I put myself out there, and was rejected, it might cause all sorts of feelings—inferiority, disappointment, failure—but I knew that all of these emotions would be temporary, and that I would get through it. What's the worst that could happen? Maybe I'd waste some unproductive time feeling sorry for myself, but that would be it. Fortunately, my pity parties are brief, and then I move on. Does rejection fuel me? To a degree, it does.

■ ■ ■ ■ ■

*"Persistence has served me well, as I got business
from clients who at one point turned me down."*
A. Lizz Patrick, Founder, Patrick Law Group

■ ■ ■ ■ ■

Oddly enough, I did not employ these techniques to grow my own business. I never asked to be considered for marketing assignments. I occasionally asked to be included when an account was up for review. There was a part of me that never felt I was good enough for consideration. But the bottom line was that I didn't know how to ask. What was the worst that could happen if I called potential clients and they turned me down? Nothing. I could move on.

Once I got myself placed on the national trade association's local board, I gradually overcame the hurdle of having most of the leaders in my industry know me. Now, what was the next thing I had to do to grow my field of influence?

The obvious next step for me was to get involved with my community. It took many years to realize that one of the reasons my business thrived was I live and work in a city that supports small business. Atlanta is a service business market that encourages entrepreneurship, particularly women and minority-owned businesses. I wanted to get involved with local organizations; I just didn't know where to start. I had to find the right guide to lead me through my options.

I noticed that a lot of executives served on non-profit boards of directors. As I was mulling this over, one of my creative staff members informed me that she was volunteering for a local group that protected women and children from domestic violence. Would I mind if she used some of the agency's resources? "No," I said, "but can you introduce me to the marketing person you're working with?" I have never been subjected to domestic violence and neither has anyone in my family, but it is a women and family issue, unfortunately. At the time, my company would periodically get involved with helping different non-profit groups. But we didn't have a formal strategy to align ourselves with specific causes. This would be our first step.

I did my homework and learned who was on the board, what their community involvement was, and whether the board was prominent enough in the community that my presence on the board would resonate. Several meetings ensued, including one with the executive director of the group. I asked, "If we provide the work you need, would you consider putting me on the board?" My asking paid off. I was appointed to the board, and I stayed through two terms. My company did exceptional pro bono work for them. I was very proud of my relationship with the organization and how I got my staff involved. Aside from donating our time to develop advertising campaigns for their fundraising efforts, my staff helped a family during the holidays by donating clothing, food, and toys for the children.

This led to my involvement with other community groups that support women, whether for diseases that directly affect women, such as breast cancer, heart disease, or multiple sclerosis, or to help women further their careers.

Want to find the perfect non-profits in your community to work with? Answer these questions:

- What groups align with your company and its mission/vision?
- Does involvement in these groups afford opportunities for your employees?
- What financial resources are required? Often a substantial contribution to the organization is required of board members.
- Who are the other board members, and what is your opportunity to get to know them?
- What in-kind services can you provide?
- What impact on the community will your involvement provide?

The process of asking for what you want

There is a process for asking for what you want. It is a somewhat organic process in that the timing of these events is fluid. Everything I wanted for The Kilgannon Group and for me (they were interchangeable) had one singular purpose: to raise my profile. You would think it would be to grow the business. Of course it was, but that was a secondary goal. If the business grew as a result of my profile being raised, that was icing on top. But what I ultimately wanted was for the business community to know my name. I figured one would beget the other.

Each time I saw an opportunity to get involved with something, I asked myself a series of questions. I recommend you do the same. Ask yourself:

- **How important is this to me?** Be prepared to articulate why you want to get involved. Most likely, someone from the governance committee will ask this question if you are seeking a board position. If you are volunteering for a committee, having a specific expertise can help. I asked myself what it would mean to the business and to me if I became involved in a particular endeavor. Can you gain recognition? Will you have the opportunity to meet important people you wouldn't ordinarily engage with?

- **Is anyone I know going to spontaneously ask me to get involved?** Don't wait around to be recruited. There are likely many other people who want the same visibility.

- **Do I know anyone who can put in a good word?** Is there anyone you know who can influence the decision to endorse you?

- **Do I know who the decision makers are?** Find out who the decision makers are and connect with them. Use the endorser's name or ask for a meeting to discuss your interest in learning more about the program, committee, non-profit board, etc.

■ **How should I behave during the initial meeting?**
Treat the meeting as if you are old friends with the decision maker, as if the two of you have something in common. Don't oversell yourself. After all, you are there to ask to get involved. Bring something to the table that will add value.

7 | BUILD CONFIDENCE

■ ■ ■ ■ ■

"No one can make you feel inferior
without your consent."
Eleanor Roosevelt

■ ■ ■ ■ ■

My desire to fit in has always motivated me. If a therapist were reading this, he or she would assume something happened in my childhood that drove this behavior. There were influential events in my childhood, but I am not, and never will be, one who wallows or engages in self-pity. So here it is in a nutshell: I am the middle child of hearing-impaired parents. I lost my older brother to Leukemia when I was 8 years old, and he was 10. A therapist once told me that I suffered from post-traumatic stress disorder at that age, but since no one had really heard of PTSD back then, there was little worry about my sister and me. I don't frequently speak about the loss of my brother. Perhaps I have survivor guilt; who knows?

Confidence is elusive. One day it is there and the next day

not. Women are more likely to have confidence issues than men; particularly in business. I have had my issues with confidence over the years; however, those issues didn't get in my way when I wanted something. A lack of confidence never prevented me from asking for what I wanted. Instead, confidence played a role in how I asked.

I think I'm articulate; however, when confidence eludes me, I become a stumbling, bumbling fool. Suddenly, how I say things—or ask for what I want—comes across weak, defensive, and unsure. Who in his or her right mind would acquiesce to the request of someone who comes across wimpy?

When a good friend of mine went through a confidence issue at work, I wanted to build her up and help raise her confidence. She had an important meeting with her managers. She had all the right technical tools to support her argument, but if she came across unsteady and not confident, they might not think she was the right person to lead. My advice? She had to have the "who cares, what's the worst that could happen?" attitude. She needed to go into the meeting without fear. Fear would cripple her before she opened her mouth.

I looked forward to hearing from her after her meeting. She phoned the next morning, relieved and happy that she got the outcome she hoped for. She confided in me that she knew how to manage her expectations of the meeting prior to going in. If she won, great; if she didn't, she knew what she would have to do. No mystery. No surprise. The fear dissipated.

A 2012 article in *Entrepreneur* magazine, titled "Why Women Business Owners Feel More Successful," cites The Hartford Financial Services Group survey of 1,004 small business owners, including 271 women and 733 men.

One of the factors that contributes to women's confidence is that they are more risk averse. About 55 percent of the women surveyed viewed themselves as conservative in taking risks in their business, compared to 47 percent of the men surveyed. Also, 80 percent of women responded that they did not think taking more risks would make them more successful.

"I have my own gut feeling about why more women are happy with their businesses: our expectations may be lower," wrote Carol Tice, the author of this article. "Fewer women go into business with dreams of building an empire. Women consider their business a success if they can be their own boss and replace former job income."

Every few years, a study called Global Entrepreneurship Monitor (GEM) issues a Women's Report. The Global Entrepreneurship Monitor project is an annual assessment of the entrepreneurial activity, aspirations, and attitudes of individuals across a wide range of countries. Some key points from its 2013 report are:

- Women often don't think they are capable of launching their own business, which is one reason there are significantly fewer female entrepreneurs than male entrepreneurs.

- Women report being generally more afraid of failure than their male counterparts.

- In all but seven of the countries surveyed, women represent a minority of the nation's entrepreneurs.

- In the U.S., there are fewer overt barriers for women to become entrepreneurs, but there are still covert barriers, specifically in gaining access to capital or winning government contracts.

I imagine the last point here validates one of many reasons female entrepreneurs wish to be part of a clearinghouse of women-owned business organizations, such as Women's Business Enterprise National Council (WBENC) and National Women Business Owners Corporation (NWBOC). These organizations exist to assure major corporations that the companies owned by the women in these groups have been properly vetted and found worthy of assignments and contracts.

■ ■ ■ ■ ■

*"I think women operate under the assumption that
it's a man's world. Women start out handicapped.
That subconscious, subversive outlook
holds women back."*
Ellen Dracos Lemming, President, Dracos-Lemming, LLC

■ ■ ■ ■ ■

Babson College professor Donna Kelley speculates that when a woman has a choice between being an employee and being a business owner she takes a greater risk by entering entrepreneurship. She has more to lose, especially when working for someone else is associated with an attractive salary, job stability, good benefits, and even high social approval.

Professor Kelley brings up the key issue of confidence here: does a woman have what it takes to overcome fear and low self-esteem to leap into her own business? Fortunately, many of us do, but unfortunately, not in big enough numbers.

Here are my suggestions for building confidence:

■ **Say "yes" more than "no."** Women have a tendency to worry too much about whether a decision is right or wrong. By not dwelling on the matter and simply taking a risk, you open yourself to possibilities. Most of the time it works out very well. When you trust your gut, and things work out, it is a big boost to your confidence.

■ **Think about your accomplishments and revel in them.** Remember how confident you felt and how people responded to you at successful junctures in your career. That should quell those negative voices in your head.

- **Stop doubting yourself.** What's the worst that could happen? Go through all the pluses and minuses of the situation that is causing a confidence dip, and project what the possible outcomes are. Nine times out of 10, you'll be able to overcome the worst that could happen.

- **Envision your success.** What will it look like, feel like? It is very helpful to see yourself in a successful mode. Others will see you as confident as long as you see yourself that way.

When my job required a lot of confidence

As head of The Kilgannon Group, I needed to appear confident during formal talks to clients, prospects, employees, and strategic and business partners. One critical part of my job in the agency was to prepare and make presentations to existing and potential clients. Making these presentations was a huge part of my image as a business owner, so I knew I had to excel here. I was never afraid to stand before people and talk, but my skills were rough around the edges. I had never been formally trained and, therefore, often tried whatever worked for me at the time.

Part of my decision to attend acting classes early in my career was because I read somewhere that great business presenters are often taught by acting coaches. I had a strange rationale that I could kill two birds with one stone: find out if I actually had any acting skills, and improve my presentation abilities at the same time. What was I thinking?

There was an upside to the acting classes and the eventual performances I participated in: learning the skills required to be a good performer gave me more confidence when presenting. It took away the fear and self-doubt I typically experienced when speaking in public. Ever since then, presentations have been a breeze, as long as I prepare and rehearse.

For entrepreneurs, having confidence and commitment when presenting is of utmost importance. This confidence was evidence of my knowledge of my craft and my credibility. Here are some of the tips I picked up, some as a result of my brief acting career:

- **No one likes PowerPoint.** The (over)use and reliance on PowerPoint can cripple presentations. It is akin to standing on the stage, script in hand, and reading to the audience. Use PowerPoint for brief statements or visuals and speak from that point only. No more than 10 words on any slide. Try it; it's very hard to do. I was also very lucky to have staff members who were particularly good at the mechanics of PowerPoint. If you have to use PowerPoint, make sure someone on your staff is skilled at it. There are dozens of classes that teach the tricks and nuances of PowerPoint. It's certainly worth the investment.

- **Rehearse, rehearse, rehearse.** You've heard that before, but it is an important part of this process, especially if you are presenting as part of a team. Much like acting, it is as important to know the cue lines of your co-presenters as it is to know your own—where you come in and go out, how to punctuate the points of the speaker prior to you, and how to set up the speaker following you. By the way, most people don't like to practice in front of each other. Often, when you call for a rehearsal, your co-presenters are nowhere to be found, or they only have five minutes. I'm convinced it's a peer embarrassment thing.

- **Determine blocking.** Know in advance where your group is sitting or standing. Should you all stand, or should you sit amongst your clients or prospects? Order the sequence of the presentation in such a fashion that different speakers are not popping up and down. Avoid the "whack-a-mole" game.

■ **Include theatre.** Every presentation needs the requisite amount of surprise and delight. When I hired experts to teach my staff, we always discussed the "theatre" surrounding the presentation. Not goofy, clown-like stuff, but ways to provide a multi-media experience for the audience. As we were in a creative business, we had to think of ways to incorporate multi-media. For example, we might use original video footage or clips from movies or TV shows to keep our audience engaged. In our business, we had creative executions to share, both on screen and on boards that we placed around the room.

■ **Know your stuff.** When I was performing, I often had a lot of lines to memorize. Over the years, I realized that I was a better auditory person and that reading and memorizing my lines was not as effective. In order to memorize my part, I would read my lines into a recording device and hit play over and over until I knew the lines by heart. I also recorded my cue lines and left enough space on the recording so I could fill in my lines. I equate this process to memorizing a song by your favorite performer. After listening to it so many times, you know the words of the song. If you have a presentation that requires a lengthy part, try this; you might be surprised at how well it works.

■ **Set up the room in advance.** As our audience came into the conference room, we made sure that the requisite material was at each person's place. For example, as we often presented in a group, we gathered everyone's business cards and placed them in an envelope at each guest's seat. One of our advisors suggested we create a one-sheet document with photos, names, and titles for each of our presenters so that at any time during the presentation, our guests could glance down and re-acquaint themselves with the current speaker. Also included was general information about our firm that served as a quick overview.

■ **Talk very little about yourself.** We only had one slide that mentioned our firm. Since we had the one-sheet at everyone's place, the general information about us filled in any blanks and did not detract from the relevant content of the presentation. I believed that since we were there to present to a client or prospect, the bulk of the presentation needed to be about them, not about us.

Although my confidence in my skill as a presenter improved as the years went by, there were times when I allowed doubt to creep in. This might have been a result of letting the competition get to me (we'll never be as good) or just having one of those days when, no matter how good the content was or how good our chances were, I was not on top of my game, no matter how hard I tried.

In one instance, just days prior to an important client meeting held at a resort with the client's customers in attendance, I found out that some medical tests I had taken came back with a serious diagnosis: I had multiple sclerosis. What seemed like a leg injury turned out to be MS. I was shocked by the news, but I didn't know enough about this nervous system disease to accurately determine what it meant for me. As a result, my mind was still spinning with news of the diagnosis by the time of the meeting. Needless to say, I didn't come across with any confidence when I spoke, and the client told me a few days later that I did not do a very good job. Although my lackluster performance didn't cause any future client issues, I left a negative impression at that meeting. I wasn't ready to tell anyone about my recent news, although it would have been an acceptable explanation. As it turned out, I continued to work closely with this client after this debacle, and all was fine, but it proved to me that I needed to pick myself up and move on.

Shortly after the presentation, I gathered the members of my management team to explain why my performance was not up to snuff. They were all sympathetic and kind, uttering words of support. But by far the funniest remark was made by one of my senior staff members who confused multiple sclerosis with muscular dystrophy and asked, "Does this mean you're one of Jerry Lewis's kids?" We all laughed until our stomachs ached. Finding the humor in serious events definitely relieves the tension. Being able to laugh at yourself is a valuable skill.

Overcoming doubt

Overthinking allows doubt to creep in, and often prevented me from moving into unchartered waters. There isn't a person out there who doesn't doubt themselves at key decision points in their personal or business life. I am the professed queen of doubt. I make a decision—whether it is to hire someone or not, or whether I want sushi or salad for lunch—and then equivocate as to whether I made the right choice.

Some decisions I never doubted, like starting my own business. There was never a flicker of "should I or shouldn't I?" For me, the timing of when to start my own business was the only uncertainty. But there was a plethora of decisions that caused a lot of angst and required a second, third, and fourth look to determine if the outcome would benefit the organization. After all, as a small business owner, I had no one to blame but myself if it didn't work out.

One case in point was a merger opportunity early in the life of the business. The owner of a graphic design firm recommended me to his client who was looking for an ad agency. This design firm only performed graphic work, not the strategic side of building the brand. I met with the client, and we agreed that my agency would develop the ad campaigns while the graphic design firm continued to complete their scope of work. The client, the graphic design firm, and my ad agency worked together to launch this company's new brand.

Things were going well when the owner of the design firm approached me about merging. Since I did not have an in-house creative department at the time, he believed a merger between our companies would be a logical fit. I didn't think it was a bad idea, but I wanted to investigate it more. What I discovered made me glad I listened to that tiny voice in my head.

The owner of the graphic design firm was a micro-manager, as well as a perfectionist. I was neither. Although I felt strongly about certain aspects of running the business, I really didn't care much if the color of my paper clips matched the color of my logo. This guy did. Our merger discussions had become serious by the time I discovered this and other issues. These traits of his did not bode well for the future of a joint relationship. I knew that if we worked together, something would eventually blow up. I had a growing staff and an important client to protect, so I called off the merger discussions. He was furious. Doubt set in, and I questioned my decision. After some quiet time and more careful thought, I realized I did the right thing. Eventually, he no longer did any work for our mutual client, but my company stayed on as their ad agency for 20 years.

■ ■ ■ ■ ■

"The unknown does not scare me. As long as I know
that what I am doing is smart and I can offer my
clients and staff the best that we can deliver at a very
fair price, then I know I'm doing the right thing."
A. Lizz Patrick, Founder, Patrick Law Group

■ ■ ■ ■ ■

This was not the first (and certainly not the last) time doubt reared its ugly head. Here is what I often do when doubt shows up:

■ **Ask for advice or verification.** Seek out professionals who are experienced in the areas that need adjusting or fixing. I am a consensus builder. Although many times in my career I was committed to making key decisions, I still wanted validation that the decision was the right one. There were advisors, key members of my staff, my business partner, and even friends who could advise me.

■ **Determine the financial implications of making the decision.** Looking at the numbers can help ease the doubt. If the numbers don't work, the consequences rise, and so does self-doubt. Numbers don't lie.

■ **Stand firm.** Evaluate all options and considerations. Once you do so, make the decision and stick with it. The people around you can sniff out doubt, so be certain of your final decision once you make it.

■ **Ask: What's the worst that could happen?** Looking at the big picture helps with the small decisions. Whenever self-doubt crept in, I repeated this phrase in my head over and over. It helped me visualize the impact. If everything worked out, great, then the decision was a good one. What if it didn't? Then I had a game plan to fix it, beforehand. I am not great on the fly, so I had to create a mental "what if" scenario.

Overcoming fear

With doubt, fear can creep in. There were a handful of times when I was truly afraid for the company and for my credibility and reputation. This fear never stopped me from moving forward, but it did snap me back to reality.

One incident in particular was a client meeting when results of a campaign needed to be presented. On this particular day, I was not at the top of my game. The meeting quickly disintegrated, not because the results of the campaign were poor, but because I hastily put together an incomplete presentation. The client immediately saw the problem and lashed out at me. I had never encountered this type of reaction before. I was silenced into doubt and the fear of losing the account. This client quickly regained his composure and apologized for his reaction and, together, we worked through the missing information. At the end of the meeting, we were both relieved, and after many mea culpas, all was forgiven. But the sting of humiliation stayed with me for days. When I arrived home that evening, I went up to my bedroom and lay down on the floor to meditate and collect myself.

I learned meditative techniques after attending a class at a spa retreat. During the session, I noticed that I could feel myself relaxing like never before. After the meditation, my head was clearer, and whatever stress I had at the time disappeared. After this difficult experience with the client, I tried it again to see if I could relax.

Meditation works differently for everyone. I knew I had to shut out all the mental noise when I was stressed and afraid. So on went the headphones and out came the yoga mat; woo-woo new age music played, and I closed my eyes and attempted to practice breathing exercises. I started these meditation sessions the correct way (I think), but sometimes I could not quiet my anxieties, and they would consume me again. However, the fact that I was on the floor, with the headset on, changed my perspective. Whatever decision or fear was brewing seemed less scary.

In addition to practicing meditation, I learned the importance of having an outside activity—physical exercise, spending time with family and friends, taking a course—that could help take my mind off my business. A good friend of mine suggested we take a knitting class. Knitting? My mother taught me to knit when I was young. She was an exceptional home-maker, a great cook, and a seamstress, and excelled in anything that involved needlepoint and knitting. Thank goodness I inherited her skill with craft-related projects. When I picked up the knitting needles in this class, it clicked. But the best thing that knitting does for me is to put me in a completely Zen-like state. It's a productive kind of meditation because it takes my mind off stressful situations and allows me to concentrate on the work at hand—literally!

Focusing on something other than the business often brings a different perspective to most any difficult situation. Perspective helps eliminate doubt and fear.

After experiencing several instances that caused fear, I recognized the sign when it appeared: my business judgment would be clouded. Personal fear issues can be overwhelming and highly distracting for entrepreneurs as well. For many, business and personal issues are very closely tied. So when there are fears related to one, the other is affected, often causing distractions. Shortly after my MS diagnosis, I was privately consumed with fear. What would become of my ability to run the company? Should I tell everyone? Once I came to grips with the MS, I conducted myself as if this was just another bump in the road. I found as long as I made no big deal of it, others relaxed. This is why taking some time to work through personal issues is key. Caring for myself, mentally or physically, for as little as a few minutes a day, really helped.

■ ■ ■ ■ ■

"I almost lost the business in 2005, but I thought, life goes on. I can dig myself out of a ditch! I do have an excavation license."
Mitzi Moore, President, Sundial Plumbing

■ ■ ■ ■ ■

Interference

Noise. There can be a lot of it. Whether inside your head or outside. Sometimes it comes from home. Other times it comes from within the company. In my case, it came from both. Most entrepreneurs—female or male—will agree that interference can be both productive and non-productive. The most damaging voice of interference can come from inside you.

Many times, I allowed my internal voice to interfere with what I knew was right and to interrupt my progress. This voice was disruptive and often contributed to my impostor complex. There are books and articles galore on this topic. Joyce Roché, author of *The Empress Has No Clothes: Conquering Self-Doubt to Achieve Success,* wrote about this in a blog for the Vistage® Organization. She describes the impostor complex as feeling like a fraud, afraid of being found out if you don't work harder and longer than everyone else. I've been there. There were many times when I believed that others were more qualified than I was, and every time I succeeded, I lacked the confidence and assurance that I could succeed again. I truly felt like an impostor.

In her blog post, Roché lists 10 ways to overcome imposter complex:

- **Don't stay silent.** One of the symptoms of imposter complex is the feeling that you are all alone. Talking about it doesn't seem right. Find someone you trust to confide in, or write about it in a diary or journal. The important point is not to keep your feelings bottled up inside.

- **See others for who they are.** Observe others you view as confident, and accept their needs and flaws. Seeing and accepting these traits in others will allow you to see yourself with compassion and understanding.

- **Learn to accept external praise and validation.** Gratefully receive compliments and put aside the tendency to respond negatively or to minimize the comment.

- **Look closely at fear.** Fear is a natural reaction to what you are experiencing. Feeling unfit is, in part, a conditioned emotional response to stress. Distinguish between the stress of new responsibilities and the conditioned response of impostor fears.

- **Question your work habits.** Consider what makes you feel worthy. Does working harder than anyone else really make you feel like less of a fake?

- **Find like-minded people.** Clarify your values and build connections with those who share them. Own who you are and what you believe in. Find people who see the real you.

- **Analyze your success.** Use logic and facts to assuage your fears. Strengthen the skill of internal validation.

- **Exercise your sense of humor.** Keep a sense of perspective and laugh as often as possible, especially at yourself.

- **Live the life you want.** Ask yourself whether you are satisfied with your life and your job. If you aren't, make a change. Living an authentic life will help minimize the worries about not fitting in.

- **Do a reality check.** Make a list of your strengths, skills, and qualities that have attracted people to you and have gotten you this far.

Although I'm a consensus builder, I don't endorse gaining group support every time a big decision needs to be made. Whenever I sought the approval of a group, I realized that most of the time I did not need their input. I knew I had made up my mind, but I wanted that extra "You go, girl," to encourage me. My internal doubt-o-meter pushed me to seek outside approval; however, I realize that I made it hard on myself by including many of them in the conversation in the first place. This was the external interference I didn't need.

An entrepreneur is always looking for the right answers. When it is not immediately apparent, the internal conversations start. Should I spend $500 on that new piece of equipment? Should I hire this questionable person? Should I opt out of that new business pitch?

When I was out of my depth in making key decisions, I delegated that responsibility to those who knew better. Which 401(k) program is best for us? Which health insurance plan should we select? I had to rely on those who knew better to make the right choice. Fortunately, the people I selected to help did a masterful job. That kind of interference is necessary and welcome.

In one instance, we had a big debate about whether to re-pitch an account that was putting all its agencies up for review. Our relationship with this account was deteriorating, and I saw little hope for us. Everyone else in my company wanted to jump in.

The process to win an account this large is arduous. Many advertising agency pitches require a lot of staff time and out-of-pocket expenses. I knew the client was including us as a courtesy, not because they thought we had a chance, but because we had worked with them for several years. In addition, the pitch was a cattle call of sorts. The client sent out the request for information (RFI) to over 25 advertising agencies across the country.

Among the many outside advisors we had was a gentleman who had a lot of experience helping agencies pitch clients. He believed—and I agreed with him—that 90 percent of the time, the client knows which agency they would like to see win the business. However, it is rare that they can just pick which firm to work with. Many corporations require more than one bid for services, particularly when the outcome means an annual expense outlay of nearly $1 million. So there has to be a bidding process. Often, the procurement or sourcing groups in major corporations get involved.

This process can take a long time and involve several steps. We went through the RFI stage and were accepted into the next round. I didn't believe we had a snowball's chance in hell to be selected, so I made the decision not to go further. Then the interference started. There were several voices weighing in, those who agreed with me and those who believed we should move forward.

I weakened and suggested we go one more round in the process. As soon as I received the eight-page document that listed all of the questions submitted by the 12 agencies left for consideration, I knew we had to decline participation. I was so sure that no amount of interference or noise would change my mind this time. This was not a good client. At times, their people were verbally abusive to my staff. They often took more than 90 days to remit payment of our invoices. They often improperly briefed us only to slam us on our execution. Why, oh why would we want to be included? I didn't want my staff to endure more of this.

I silenced all the voices, called the client, and advised them that we would not participate. I was polite, yet firm, when I removed my agency from consideration. I graciously thanked them, though. No need to burn a bridge. As it turned out, my consultant was right. The client wanted to work with a particular firm, which was ultimately awarded the business. As my friend and business partner, Mike Reineck likes to say: *quelle surprise!*

THE LESSON:

- **Go with your gut. Your inner voice has gotten you this far, and if it has not let you down before, chances are you can trust it.**

- **There will always be outside noise. Everyone claims to be an expert on your business. Recognize who is there to help you move forward, and who just likes to talk.**

- **There will be mistakes. There will be times when you do not make the right decision. But failure is a good thing, not a bad omen. You've heard it time and again: failure is part of success. Learn from it, remember it, and move on.**

8 | IMAGE IS EVERYTHING?

■ ■ ■ ■ ■

"Everywhere I've been today there's always been something wrong—too young, too old, too short, too tall. Whatever the exception is, I can fix it. I can be older, I can be taller, I can be anything."
Michael J. Fox, as Brantley Foster, in *The Secret of My Success*

■ ■ ■ ■ ■

I was in my mid-20s when I moved to Atlanta, and I hadn't yet come into my own style; actually, I never had a style. In Atlanta, I wanted to fit in more with the fashion of the professional women around me. I noticed they looked very put together. I worked with a female client who always dressed to the nines. During one of my visits with her, I couldn't help but notice that the lining of her jacket matched her skirt, and that blew me away. I didn't know where to start to shop like that; I was clueless.

From my perspective at the time, looking like this would provide an advantage with influential people. It seemed to me that important executives responded to (and respected) women who had a more put-together look. My interpretation was—and still is—that there is a perception that if a woman looks professionally stylish, there is likely to be substance there. True or not, those who matter in business are more likely to give you an audience, whether you are networking, selling something, or interviewing for a job. You have to look professionally put together.

Adopting this style and way of life did not come naturally for me. While the women in my life when I was growing up were meticulous about their style and look, I did not feel comfortable, or quite frankly, look good in a lot of clothes. I was a chubby kid and I dressed like one. I was never fat, but rather thick looking. Everyone around me was small or in proportion—I was bottom heavy, or so I thought—and nothing looked as good on me, in my opinion. Now, when I look at photos of myself, I see what I felt at the time. In two words: awkward and uncomfortable.

Image is another issue tied to confidence. Whenever I didn't like the way I looked or felt, I knew it was obvious; I came across as less than confident. Although I was not afraid to meet or talk to people, I lacked confidence when it came to how I looked. So I went on a campaign to go to the most expensive shops and buy clothing I thought was more appropriate. I also had weekly manicures and went to the hairdresser often. In short, I believed I needed to transform to be accepted and blend in.

■ ■ ■ ■ ■

"I began to become uncomfortable as the firm grew. I never fit in 100 percent. I looked the part, but I was not like many of the other female partners who were 'sorority little sisters' to this big fraternity-like, male-dominated firm. I started questioning many of the decisions that were made."

A. Lizz Patrick, Founder, Patrick Law Group

■ ■ ■ ■ ■

Over the years, dress styles and codes relaxed, particularly in the creative business environment of an ad agency. Many organizations went from business casual Fridays to business casual every day. Even major, conservative corporations now allow for this type of dress code. However, there is a slightly different code for women in organizations when it comes to business casual. Walk into any corporate environment today, and you are likely to see women who wear more professional attire than their male counterparts.

I relaxed our dress codes as The Kilgannon Group matured; however, I wanted client-facing managers to "dress for their day." That simply meant that if there were client meetings—in or out of the office—business dress was required. For men, this meant nice pants, a dress shirt or a well-pressed golf shirt (depending on how the client organization dressed), a blazer if needed, and nice shoes. For women, it was dressier. As we were in a creative business, it wasn't necessary for women to dress like bankers. Nice slacks or skirt, a blouse, sometimes a blazer, perhaps a dress, and nice accessories were my interpretation of acceptable.

What I did not expect was how many young women had no idea how to dress for client meetings, interviews, or presentations. The confusion might have been the result of a generational difference from my baby boomer sensibilities, or simply that these young women were never taught what was appropriate attire for business. It was probably a combination of both.

I started to notice deterioration in the attire of many of the young women who worked at the agency. It seemed as if they all wore sloppy, old jeans every day. Worse, when the popular style was to show off a woman's midriff, many of these young women did just that. To add more fuel to the fire, those who were well endowed wore tops with plunging necklines that revealed too much cleavage. I have to confess this was not obvious to me until one of my female managers discreetly told me she noticed that the casual attire policy we put in place was not working. Suddenly, I noticed the flaws in everyone's clothing. Even the guys in our office were slacking off.

I phoned a friend to ask for advice. She ran a successful public relations firm, and months earlier had hired a professional stylist to teach her staff how to dress appropriately for different business occasions. This included client meetings, important internal meetings, dinners, events, and even what to pack for business trips. I hired this style professional to give a presentation to the women in my company. I told the women on my staff that I was bringing in a stylist as a special perk for them, and I would pay for her time to meet with each of them individually, so she could advise them on their individual look. Whew! That worked.

A FEW TIPS ABOUT DRESS CODE:

- **If the attire of your staff is a problem, hire a professional to assist.**

- **Encourage your staff to dress like the culture of your client or strategic partner organization. These stakeholders have to see you as one of their own, so it's important to fit in during any circumstance.**

Suddenly, everyone dressed better, and the sloppy jeans, midriff-baring, overt cleavage look started to go away. We even assigned one of our office managers to secretly police our dress code. If someone was out of line, his or her manager was immediately informed, and the offender was sent home to change. Who knew that all we needed was a little intervention?

9 | KEEP LEARNING

■ ■ ■ ■ ■

"Why-why-why? ...
Ask it of everything your mind touches,
and let you mind touch everything!"
Ann Fairbairn

■ ■ ■ ■ ■

I was self-conscious of not having a college degree. Not having that sheepskin contributed to the impostor complex I couldn't shake. What if someone found out? I was surrounded by college graduates and MBAs and wanted badly to fit into that club. Women would speak of sororities, men of fraternities. I worried that one of them might ask about my college experience. So I sought another route: professional education.

I convinced myself that being exposed to as many professional development opportunities as possible would fill the gap. I sought out continuing education opportunities in my field of direct and integrated marketing. I also researched relevant leadership programs to improve my skill in this area.

I've always felt I needed leadership training. In many large corporations, there are programs to enhance leadership skills for up-and-coming managers. As an entrepreneur, I was leading by the seat of my pants, and I thought there might be more to effective leadership than what I was demonstrating.

Who is the perfect candidate for leadership training? In my opinion, it is someone who has a natural curiosity, is never satisfied with the status quo, and has a fear of failure. *Note:* If you are a seller of leadership training programs, read this carefully; I am describing your perfect prospect!

I looked for the ideal leadership program that would resonate with me. Many addressed various leadership styles and techniques, and I learned at least one new technique at each training session. I often returned from leadership training jazzed up to implement one or more of the recommended management techniques in hopes of inspiring my staff. Did they work? Um, you'd have to ask the staff I led over the years. In my opinion, many of these approaches never stuck. There was a certain rhythm to the company, and whenever I attempted to shift it after returning from one of these programs, everyone, including me, got out of whack. It just wasn't us, no matter how I tried to force it. In retrospect, I can see that we were not big change advocates. If it wasn't broken, why fix it?

■ ■ ■ ■ ■

"When a client canceled a contract, I wanted to crawl into the fetal position. One of my staff told me to lead them. That was a big wake up call."
Stacy Williams, President, Prominent Placement, Inc.

■ ■ ■ ■ ■

Part of what drove me to these programs was the opportunity to expand my network. I wanted to know more people, and I wanted them to know me. Where else would I get the exposure to people at my level or above from large and small organizations around the country?

When there was no money in the budget to pay for the training, I paid out of my own pocket. Why? Maybe it was my endless curiosity, but it was also because these programs were important to me. I could continue to become more credible and even, perhaps, be a better marketer and leader, so it didn't matter what the cost was. Each leadership program I was involved with cost thousands of dollars. I have never regretted spending company money, or my own, on any of them. This was always money well spent.

After I was in business for several years, I learned about a program run out of the University of Missouri, Kansas City. It was an advanced certificate program in direct marketing taught by leaders in the industry. This was a three-week program, broken down into one-week segments over the course of six months. Without much thought, and despite the high price tag, I signed up. I wanted to do it so I could excel in this, my designated field of marketing. I could include it as part of my education credentials.

A few things resulted from this experience: 1) I learned a lot more than I anticipated about the discipline of direct marketing, which helped my confidence, 2) I met very interesting people from around the country in the same field of study, 3) I met and interacted with well-known educators, practitioners, and writers of the discipline, and 4) I fell in love with Kansas City.

This was not enough, however, to satisfy my need to be among the leaders of the pack in my field. Once I began to practice integrated marketing communications (IMC), I wanted to get even better at it. There are lots of claims as to where IMC originated. Since I followed the teaching of Don Schultz, PhD and his academic program, I signed up to attend a certificate program at Northwestern University's Medill School of Journalism, where he was one of the leading experts.

During this three-day program, I studied with marketing

professionals from around the country. I attended the program with one of my account managers, and we learned how different marketing disciplines worked together to achieve sales results. Significant takeaways were the database and analytic components, which set this discipline apart from its general marketing cousins. It was a fascinating three days, and having attended the class provided me, and my company, the credibility I craved with employees, potential employees, clients, prospects, and industry peers.

My industry trade association, The American Association of Advertising Agencies, offered an executive training program aimed at the most senior managers in advertising agencies. This was also a program I felt I needed to attend for a couple of reasons: it taught attendees about running an agency, and it addressed issues that only the most senior executives deal with.

The participants ran mock agencies replete with successes, challenges, and failures. This program was limited to 21 attendees who were then broken into three teams. The lessons learned were invaluable and immediately applicable to the businesses all of us were returning to. Most who attended were senior managers of large, multinational organizations, rather than entrepreneurs running their own firms. All of the attendees brought their best thinking and business problem-solving skills to the table. I learned that, despite my fears and doubts, I knew what I was doing when it came to running an agency; this program and related lessons provided important validation.

The Cadillac of the leadership programs for me was outside of my industry. It was a community, top-level leadership program that was developed for executives in Atlanta. I had read about this program and watched some of my colleagues go through it. This program only accepts the crème de la crème of the local business community. I wanted to be considered part of this elite group.

■ ■ ■ ■ ■

"I read a lot and always sought new information
about my field. I was never satisfied. The combination
of knowledge plus passion fueled me."
A. Lizz Patrick, Founder, Patrick Law Group

■ ■ ■ ■ ■

I looked into this program and thought that it might be over my head. When I first looked at the application, I immediately thought it was not for me because I didn't think I had the breadth of community service work required. I was intimidated by the onerous application process; I felt as if I was submitting an application to a higher education program. So I moved on.

Several years later, I was introduced to the woman in charge of this community-based leadership program at an annual event celebrating "Women of Excellence." The honorees were selected by a local business publication, and I had the pleasure of being recognized as one of these women. At the time I was featured in the publication, the recognition program was called "Divas of the Business Community." They since regained their senses and now refer to it as "Women of Excellence."

I knew some of the women through my board work at local charitable organizations. When I was introduced to the head of the leadership program, she encouraged me to apply to the next class. Now, just to fill you in, this nine-month program is generally a time suck that participants have to commit to along with everything else they do. Although I was warned about this, all I thought about was being accepted. The task, then, was how to not sound like a total idiot in the application write-up.

After thinking about it for a while, I dove in. I started to fill out the application and decided I had to be perfectly honest in every section. If they did not accept me because I didn't finish college or did not have an advanced degree, well, I would have to live with that. In the past, I often glossed over the fact that I never finished college. In job applications or on resumes I would put down the name of the university I attended, the number of years I was there, and the degree I was going for. Here, I had to be as transparent as possible.

I wanted to answer the questions correctly and include content that would resonate with the selection committee. I sought the help of others who had been through the application process. On several occasions people told me that if I was not selected, I should try again next year. "No way," I thought. "This is just too hard." I was firm in my commitment that this was my one and only attempt.

I must have read the completed application dozens of times before submitting it. I reviewed many of the key points with some of my business advisors to gauge their reactions. Then I tweaked it until I knew there was no more editing to be done. At some point, I had to let it go. I crossed my fingers, hit submit, and it was gone.

The selection process is a long one. I submitted in late fall and didn't hear anything until early spring the following year. Over 300 applications are submitted each year, which then gets narrowed down to 100 to 125 candidates who move on to round two. At the end of the process they offer slots to only 75 or 80 of the candidates for the upcoming class. The final decision comes later that spring. The first group of candidates receives a congratulations letter for making it to the next round. These candidates then must contact specific alumni who have agreed in advance to be part of the selection process. The fate of the candidate is partly in these people's hands.

Here's the bottom line: whoever is going to endorse you to move forward has got to like you. Period. If you cannot relate to this alum/influencer, you are done. Toast. Finito. So I had to bring my sunniest of personalities (I do have several, you know!) and pray I wouldn't be asked anything "technical." I also had to have the language right when asked why I wanted to be a part of this program.

Fortune smiled on me. The alumni member selected to interview me was a lovely woman, an attorney who had been through the leadership program a few years before. During our meeting, we discovered we had lots in common, most notably our mutual love of theatre. The luncheon was quickly coming to an end when she mentioned that she would be remiss if she didn't ask me any of the questions that she was charged to ask, so she threw some benign questions at me that I easily answered. Fast forward two months, and I received a call from one of the leaders in the community who informed me that I had been accepted into the following year's class.

I went through the program, and it had to be one of the most gratifying leadership learning experiences I have ever been through. It opened my eyes about my community, the people in it, and what my city is all about. But the most valuable gifts I received were the indelible friendships I made. The doors that have opened to me since are remarkable. As to the leadership training itself, well, quite frankly that's not truly why I did the program. It really was to meet new and different people—to have business and personal relationships that could affect my personal and professional development.

In the end, that program more than accomplished what I needed and wished for at the time. Influential executives in large and small organizations learned about me as I learned about them. These were executives in finance and operations; many were attorneys, judges, and physicians. Where else would I have the opportunity to meet and get to know these remarkable people?

How to find the right continuing education and leadership programs:

- If you are a member of a trade association, look into the continuing education programs at your disposal. See if they can advance your skill set and reputation.

- If your firm is a member of WBENC, NWBOC, or any of the female enterprise organizations, they often have annual meetings, webinars, and LinkedIn groups where you can learn of advanced leadership programs.

- Consult with your peers. Like-minded entrepreneurs seek out leadership programs. Perhaps they can lead you to one.

- Many major university systems have continuing education programs geared to business professionals. Look into your local university system for more information.

- Executive MBA programs are held in the evenings and on weekends. Although they can be costly, this might be the right move to give you and your business a leg up. Sometimes these programs are online, affording you more flexibility than having to attend at a physical location.

- Does your community have a leadership program for the city's top business professionals? Many cities around the country have a similar program to the one I attended.

VALUE
YOUR TRUSTED
10 | ADVISORS

■ ■ ■ ■ ■

"Watch, listen, and learn.
You can't know it all yourself. Anyone who thinks
they do is destined for mediocrity."
Donald Trump

■ ■ ■ ■ ■

I know where I am weak and where I excel. I also know what I do not know. I trusted there were others who could help move my company forward in areas where I lacked the know-how. So, for the sake of transparency, here is where I often needed help:

Financials. The math thing always got to me. Reading financial statements is like reading a foreign language. Plus, everyone in business today uses different language to describe the same thing. Is it revenue or gross profit? Is it income or net sales? I often needed a translator. Eventually, after many years of good counsel, I could figure out what was good and what was not.

Selling. I am good at sales, but not at selling. I'm good at forming relationships, but struggle to get them started under pressure. I hate cold calling. There are very few businesses where cold calling actually works, and mine was not one of them. For many clients, choosing an ad agency is part beauty contest, part relationship. Plus, clients don't change ad agencies every week. Most of the time, they stay with a firm for years. Landing a client is all about being at the right place at the right time.

Human resources. I had very good relationships with most members of my staff, but I was a semi-adequate HR person. When the company was small, I hired and fired, chose health care plans, determined company policies, and oversaw performance reviews. As the company increased in staff size, I quickly grew to dislike all of these tasks because there was so much to do, and I felt it was getting away from me.

Planning. I am a very good strategic business planner ... for clients. I was not very good at it for my own company. Maybe I was too close to it and could never see beyond our capabilities. I thought bringing in consultants to help us plan for growth would help, but I often met with skepticism from my business partners or my staff. So I ran a reactionary organization. Whatever happened, we would deal with it as it came. This worked for a period of time, but as the business grew, I knew I needed more of a vision for the business. Our focus sharpened as we began to plan for our niche. Our brand was built around our knowledge of business-to-business marketing, so we capitalized on that.

Marketing. Although this is my field, I was aware that

I didn't know everything about marketing. This aspect of business is constantly evolving. I wanted to know the latest, greatest, most compelling twist on the discipline that could help me sell to prospects, or better yet, bring new concepts to my clients.

Having credibility was important to me, and I sought to establish it regularly. Still, I had to seek insight and advice from experts in the areas where my own knowledge could take the company only so far.

Seek help

One character trait that has worked to my advantage is that I was never afraid to ask for help. If there was someone endorsed by a legitimate source in any of the aforementioned areas, or someone who was well respected in his or her industry, I figured out a way to bring in that person.

Seeking help is sometimes daunting. You think you've got it all figured out, when you really don't. You might not know you need help or where to get it. This was likely what Aunt Carol went through as her business grew. The difference between us is that I reached out for help. I saw no evidence that she did.

Early on, I realized that, in order to grow, I had to add expertise to support my limitations. It was time to start bringing in partners, outside vendors, and staff that added credibility to the company.

■ ■ ■ ■ ■

"At first, I was kicking and screaming against advisors.
Now, I seek them out and welcome their advice."
Stacy Williams, President, Prominent Placement, Inc.

■ ■ ■ ■ ■

Once I got into the professional world, I sought advice, mostly from experts who knew more about running a business than I did. In all my years of relying on the counsel of trusted mentors, I learned that there are two types of advisors: 1) those who are close to you—I'll call them insiders—and, 2) those who you bring in from the outside—let's be original and call them outsiders. Whether they are inside or outside is determined by one fact: inside is free and outside is not.

Outside advisors cost money, and they often come at a high price, particularly when they are well known and have a following. I looked to my own industry to point me in the right direction for the perfect advisor. After all, if I was bringing in outside advisors, they had to know the inner workings of our industry, including the quirks.

At the start of my entrepreneurial venture, my wonderful husband (an inside advisor) attempted to advise me on financial matters. Bob was a corporate banker, now retired, and he knows numbers better than I do. I will also confess that it is tough to get, take, and apply advice from someone who is emotionally invested in you. Bob was a big help in looking at balance sheets and income statements. "Honey," he would say, "none of this seems to be working. You're not running a financially sound business."

"Huh?" I mumbled, feeling intimidated and searching for some sort of defensive response.

"You're spending more money than you're earning, and you're paying your bills with borrowed money. You know that's not a good thing, don't you?"

"Huh?" I squeaked. During this time, whenever anyone, especially Bob, questioned me about the numbers, I was immediately struck dumb. I mean super dumb.

I didn't know where to turn. I had an accounting firm that did not specialize in ad agency financials. They produced the requisite financial statements each month, but didn't offer any meaningful advice. Around this time I attended a luncheon featuring a speaker who was knowledgeable about advertising agency finances. The presentation made so much sense that I approached the speaker afterwards and set up a meeting.

This meeting was the beginning of a 20-plus year relationship with my business partner and friend, Michael Reineck, an inside/outside advisor (if there is such a thing). Mike is a seasoned CPA, MBA, and was CFO of a well-known Atlanta ad agency. Here, finally, was someone who had financial expertise with advertising agencies. He was also trained by the very best the industry had to offer, Harry Paster, a long-time financial expert from our national trade association.

Mike taught me how to run a financially well-managed business. The key for me was being willing to open up and let someone be my teacher. I know many entrepreneurs who had very good advisors, but because they were not open to listening and making difficult decisions, they failed. I knew that I needed help with the financials, and that help was critical for me in becoming fiscally responsible.

I have been blessed with his counsel for more than 20 years. Mike has worked with many small marketing communications firms over the years, but he found his place at The Kilgannon Group because he found the ideal student: me. He was a tough taskmaster when it came to anything to do with making sure the numbers worked. I listened to nearly everything he taught me. Yes, there were times when I was resentful of the financial skew he put on everything we did. But 99 percent of the time, he did so with an eye towards the financial health and profitability of the firm.

Mike's true value to me was his honesty about the state of our financials. When the Great Recession of 2008 hit, the agency was in good financial shape. We had built up enough working capital in the business over the previous seven years to withstand an economic downturn. We just didn't know it would last as long as it did.

Not only were financials a thorn in my side, so was

marketing my own company. As fate would have it, I found someone I knew could help me be a better marketer. I was at a conference and stepped into a session led by an academic who used to be a professional in the marketing field. As he talked about his philosophy and approach to the business of marketing, I was moved. It was as if I was struck by a thunderbolt. He preached a methodology that starts from the very essence of direct marketing and expands to include other forms of communications. The heart of this approach revolves around return on marketing investment, and I'm a big believer in that concept. I believed this was the approach to take because (a) I completely understood what he was teaching, and (b) I was convinced this was the right way to help market any company.

For the next several years, I became a "groupie" of this academic, Dr. Don Schultz (an inside advisor). Don played a key role in the development of the Integrated Marketing unit of the Medill School of Journalism at Northwestern University outside of Chicago. I attended many of the conferences he conducted all over the country. I even convinced one of my clients to join me at a conference. It was there that we decided that Don could be an advisor to his company, and by extension, mine. Don was a rock star to me, and now I was going to learn directly from the master.

Don and his wife, Heidi—his business partner—helped several of my clients. We worked together to help my clients grow their businesses through his concept of integrated marketing. I was a big believer then, and even more so now, that Don's revolutionary approach was the best way for my clients to realize success in their marketing campaigns. I believe that Don saw the digital future before digital marketing took hold.

When Don and Heidi completed their second textbook on integrated marketing, they asked if they could put me in their book. They did, and it is one of the greatest honors I've ever had. I can safely say that Don was responsible for shaping my marketing planning approach, and to this day I claim him as one of my most influential advisors.

How to get the most from advisors:

Over the years, I received a lot of advice from both inside and outside advisors. Here are my recommend-dations for when to listen and implement, and when to just listen.

- **Get your money's worth.** When engaging outside advisors, consider the following: 1) Is the expense in your budget? 2) Check their references and ask them: Did you get your money's worth? Are you imple-menting the advisor's recommendations? How was the cultural fit for your company? Did your staff buy into the need for this advisor?

- **Get buy-in from staff.** Whether someone is coming in to help with your financial picture or any operational process, chances are everyone in the organization will be affected. Altering a process or processes will only be effective if everyone sees the need. If only the CEO wants to implement something new for the sake of change, chances are weak that the organ-ization will accept it. Involving staff in your advisor's plan is critical.

- **Assess the need for an advisor.** Look within the organization to determine if an outside advisor is actually needed. Take a look inside your company to see if you have someone who can implement or teach others how to adapt to a new approach.

- **Depend on your industry for solid referrals.** I was very dependent on our national trade organization to lead me to the correct advisor. They rarely let me down and often opened the door to interesting and knowledgeable experts. If I found a need for someone outside my industry, I relied on advice from well-respected business leaders in my community.

KNOW THE BUSINESS OF
11 | YOUR BUSINESS

■ ■ ■ ■ ■

"Nothing will work unless you do."
Maya Angelou

■ ■ ■ ■ ■

I am a student of the advertising agency business. For me, it was important to learn the best practices of running the business and to figure out what was behind the curtain on the operations side. I wanted to learn about the agency disciplines I knew nothing about: creative, media, project management, and human resources. I also wanted to know how to create a brand for the agency. Here I was, a professional in the area of branding for others, but very often, I was the shoemaker who went around with holes in my shoes.

Because I had experience working for other agencies, I knew the value of these specialty areas, but I did not know how to manage them. I went without in-house expertise in the creative and media areas for the first nine years in business. Once The Kilgannon Group started to build these areas within the agency, I recruited very talented people to run these groups. What they did and how they did it still held a certain amount of mystery to me, but once they were on staff I had to learn.

My business partners were familiar with having leaders in the areas of creative and media at the time, so they brought me up to speed as best they could. But they approached these disciplines with an account management and financial perspective. Had either of them been a creative or media leader in the past, I probably would have had a slightly different view on how to manage these groups.

I learned a lot about running my business from my industry peer groups. I sought advice from my ad agency friends around the country about how they managed various disciplines within their agencies. Some of them established teams to work on client initiatives. These teams were comprised of an account manager, a media person, and a creative team. But The Kilgannon Group was never large enough and never had enough staff in each of these areas to make the team approach work. It was best to let the managers run their individual groups on behalf of our clients.

I spent a lot of time with Mike learning how to be as accountable as possible to our clients, from a fiduciary viewpoint. If the clients were entrusting us with a lot of their budget money—sometimes millions of dollars—we had to make sure we managed the money responsibly.

In the advertising agency business, revenue consists of a variety of sources. Often a firm charges staff time by the hour. For larger, annual marketing programs, the client prefers to pay a monthly fee in lieu of hourly rates. If a client wishes the agency to order and place ads in publications or on TV or radio, even if they place digital ads, the agency can be compensated on a percentage of the total media spend. In some circumstances, the agency is compensated with an hourly fee, or project fee, for the creative staff that develops the work.

Because most of the larger amounts were spent with outside

vendors, we implemented a reconciliation process to make sure the money budgeted for media expenditures was for space and/or time that actually ran. This required a lot of work from our administrative and media staff. If we discovered that an ad was ordered, but not run (for whatever reason), our staff was on the phone obtaining "make goods," or a rebate of some kind. I learned that when an order is placed, follow-up is critical to ensure that the order is fulfilled. Many media properties will provide proof as part of their invoice, but some do not. In going through all of this, we remained diligently honest in the care of our clients' funds.

I knew nothing of this when I started my business. I quickly developed an understanding of how we made our money on the media side of the business. As the business model for compensation for media changed over the years, it was important to reframe the compensation for the media department's time.

Financial projections for the revenue generated by the creative staff dictated how many creative people to have. The strength of our creative output depended on the quality of that staff. Since creative is the primary product an ad agency sells, it is very important to have a talented staff. And they come at a significant cost.

I was never great at managing creative leaders. We spoke different languages, and I struggled with grasping their point-of-view. It was a typical left-brain/right-brain challenge. I was impatient when presented with grandiose ideas that I knew the client could not afford, and I knit-picked at nuances in strategy briefs. Some of my "interpreters" helped see me through difficult creative input sessions, but eventually, I removed myself for the sake of the team.

As our agency grew and we added business and staff, the responsibilities on the operations side grew. My focus shifted to business development, getting frequent updates on client business, attending meetings with managers and with clients, and working closely with Mike on running the company. The adage "jack of all trades, master of none" was becoming more applicable to me every day.

Human resources became an onerous task that involved so many forms, as well as discussions about benefits, employee issues, and task-oriented projects. I hated it. Although I liked the interviewing process and making job offers, I knew a slew of paperwork would follow. Not my favorite thing.

Oddly enough, I never was afraid to let people go. Whether they needed to go due to performance issues, or for any other reason, having those conversations was never difficult. I always hoped that the employee would not get emotional, but often they did. I was sympathetic, but it was no secret that I had a low tolerance for emotional reactions. I lived by the line delivered by Tom Hanks in *A League of Their Own:* "There's no crying in baseball!"

As The Kilgannon Group gained recognition in the industry, and I tried to meet my obligations as business development director, it became apparent that we had a weakness in positioning the agency brand. Who were we? What did we stand for? What was our point of differentiation? How could we distinguish ourselves during competitive pitches?

Like many firms, we were convinced that a tagline would say it all for us. By the way, if a client suggested that a tagline could be their brand position, we convinced them otherwise. When Rick McReynolds became my business partner in 1997, the creative director we hired gave us the tagline "an agency," and we approved it. Really? We let that happen? Yep.

As the years went by, we continuously struggled with this problem. It became a thorn in our side. Every time we put a new business presentation together, we came up with something we thought would separate us from the pack. For a long time, we settled on "Find. Keep. Grow." This came directly out of my integrated marketing training. Nothing sexy about it, but it was a statement we could stand behind and explain.

Mike and I met Tim Williams (an outside advisor), a

consultant to the marketing communications industry. Like Don Schultz, Tim was a seasoned advertising agency professional. He knew the inside of an agency, having been a principal at several of them.

Eventually, Tim saw the need to become a consultant to the business when he realized the lack of branding work agencies were doing for themselves. When we invited him to meet with us, he brought with him his recent book, *Stand for Your Brand.* It was written specifically for companies like mine.

We had no defined brand, and we were safely ensconced in that famous "middle" area that Tim refers to as the "general market." His insight confirmed that there was nothing to distinguish us from any other ad agency. Yet, we had very different offerings that set us apart. Our biggest problem was that we were not communicating them. Tim helped us to recognize and embrace those unique traits.

It cost us a lot of money to bring Tim in as one of our outside advisors, and we didn't do it just once; we brought him in on several occasions. I was a consensus builder when Tim was around. I wanted everyone on my senior staff to be on board with everything he advised. Unfortunately, we were not all on the same page.

After a series of sessions with Tim, we realized that the client brands we represented were not all well-known names. Most of them were in specific industry categories and marketed primarily in the business-to-business space. The average consumer would know few of them. Most of these client brands flew under the radar, even though they were very successful companies.

When we came to this realization, our creative team developed the phrase "low-flying brands." This was something we could hang our hat on. If a potential client wanted to build their brand, we empathized and explained that we knew how to take on that challenge, because we had the case histories and a track record of working with others who had the same issues.

We ran with that brand position for the next several years. Eventually, it became polarizing (not a bad thing, by the way), mostly for our internal staff. Most of them wanted to represent better-known companies, and they believed our positioning isolated us from companies that didn't connect with low-flying brands. Although we didn't walk away from clients that were attracted to that positioning, we did remove it as an agency descriptor line.

In the end, we all believed theoretically in what Tim taught us, but we had a difficult time implementing some of his teachings. I was not brave enough to demand that we immediately change as drastically as was necessary. There were many opposing voices that bombarded me for days following a Tim Williams visit. What Tim was teaching us seemed too radical a shift at the time. He was a visionary who viewed the advertising industry through a different pair of glasses. He attempted to change a business model that was more than a century old and needed to evolve to keep up with the emerging media landscape, client accountability demands, and the pressures of running a profitable business.

Minding our Ps and Qs

An important part of our business was to ensure that we were responsible with the appropriate paperwork to execute campaigns on behalf of our clients. We insisted that all forms were signed, from purchase orders to cost estimates to letters of agreement.

All too often, in professional services businesses like ours, verbal approvals serve as authorization to make large purchases on behalf of clients. I had heard of too many instances where verbal approvals were negated due to a difference in understanding what the commitment was. Many of my agency friends and clients were left holding the (empty) bag because they proceeded without signed authorization.

When a relationship moves forward with a client, a binding, legal agreement must be reached to protect the company from any liability that may occur. These agreements came in a variety of forms. Sometimes we issued cost estimates that detailed all the inside and outside expenses with accompanying payment terms. Oftentimes, and wherever possible, there was either a simple letter of agreement or a full-blown contract that enumerated the details of payment terms, confidentiality, ownership of the work product, liability, and indemnity.

Mike and I—and eventually, all of our account managers—made sure that every client understood the necessary paperwork to ensue each assignment. We were diligent in providing clients with up-to-date budget spreadsheets to ensure the client was clear about what they committed to spend and what actually came in as a final expense. Annual reconciliations followed.

In one new-business meeting, the first question the prospect asked me was whether or not I had a line of credit. I had never been asked that as the first question out of the gate, but within short order, I knew why. He had just ended a relationship with an agency that did not use his money to pay media charges for which the client had committed. The agency used the money to pay other, non-client related, expenses, and eventually the media started to call the client directly to ask for payment. This client wanted to be sure any monies paid to us for outside expense commitments were used appropriately. We promised that we would set up very tight controls for him: a separate bank account that we both had access to, so he could see the activities in and out of the account. We implemented these controls and had a very successful five-year relationship with the client.

We put other safeguards in place to minimize our exposure. The last thing we wanted was to be put in a negative cash flow position, should the client not pay or refute an expense. There was the periodic error made by one of the parties involved which did force us to cover expenses; however, these incidents were few and far between.

THE LESSON:

- Understand how your business makes money. Develop a working knowledge of your income statement, and at year-end, decide if you need to leave money in the business.

- Put checks and balances in place. This ensures you and your clients are kept legally and financially secure.

- Stay on top of your receivables. I was a very determined bill collector if an invoice lagged too long.

- Involve your staff. Client-facing staff should be included in all matters of compliance paperwork.

12 | BUSINESS PARTNERS— PROS AND CONS

■ ■ ■ ■ ■

*"Having a partner definitely allows you
to take more risks."*
Arianna Huffington, Co-founder, *The Huffington Post*

■ ■ ■ ■ ■

When I started the business in 1988, I envisioned myself running the company on my own. I did not see the possibility of a legal business partnership. I believed I'd go solo until someone saw fit to purchase the company.

As the company grew and added larger clients, I needed someone with more expertise than I had in the area of strategic marketing. My clients were requiring more from us than creating and executing ads, brochures, and direct mail campaigns. I had to find someone who could advise me—maybe even work for me—who had these specific skills.

As fate would have it, Rick McReynolds and I knew each other through the local Ad Club. At a luncheon we both attended, I learned that he had retired from the agency he had been with and was available to help me. We soon struck an agreement, and after the first year of working together, we talked about becoming partners.

During this time, Mike Reineck was my freelance CFO and business advisor. He supported my decision to partner with Rick, and walked me through the requirements of bringing Rick on as a principal shareholder in The Kilgannon Group.

We put a value on the company and set the company's price per share.

(l to r): Mike Reineck, Michael Hammond (founding client, The Fund), Rena Kilgannon, Rick McReynolds

The next step was to determine the percentage each of us would own. I didn't feel comfortable giving up majority control since I was the company's founder and I still wanted final say on all major decisions.

After nine years of running the business by myself, I had a partner. Rick played a critical role in the company's growth. He was responsible for moving us from a five-person, virtual company to a more established full-service ad agency. He brought us from a disbanded group of freelancers organized by my internal team to a more credible, competitive company that was a serious contender for winning new clients. He also assumed responsibility for overseeing the marketing direction for most of our accounts.

I didn't mind working closely with someone who shared the responsibility of running the company. It was a relief to have Rick there to brainstorm and commiserate with. Plus, it didn't hurt that we had increased success winning business because of his expertise.

Shortly after Rick and I became partners, Mike expressed interest in joining us, and both Rick and I agreed. So I took on two business partners in a matter of a few years. Each of us had distinct responsibilities, and we rarely found ourselves in disagreement. After four years with us, Rick fully retired. Although we were sad to see him leave, he left his mark by putting us on a path towards success.

Choose the right partner

Taking on a business partner is akin to a long-term personal relationship, like marriage.

There has to be trust, mutual respect, and shared goals, as well as a genuine effort to be kind to and considerate of each other. All of these characteristics help partners maintain an atmosphere of honesty and openness when facing tough decisions.

Having a shared vision is the most important part of a successful partnership. Establishing the vision early on is critical to ensuring that the company moves in the right direction.

Kilgannon Group partners (l to r): Mike Reineck,
Rena Kilgannon, Rick McReynolds

Oftentimes partnerships don't work because there is a prior personal relationship. Perhaps two or more friends, family members, or long-time work colleagues believe they can make a partnership work. Although this sometimes goes well, such partnerships often fail due to baggage that's brought into the professional relationship, usually having nothing to do with the business venture.

I've also witnessed partnerships that develop when a potential partner promises added revenue in exchange for ownership rights in the company. This type of arrangement can mean compromises the founder or owner does not expect. Sometimes the potential partner wants the account he or she has brought in to be treated differently than the legacy business the company was established on. Other times promises to new clients are made that can't be kept.

In other cases, partners come on board in exchange for sweat equity that they infuse into the company. I am completely opposed to this type of arrangement. I learned early on that there is no such thing as sweat equity. Exchanging labor and time for company shares short-changes the founder. If the owner of the business has invested money, then anyone who wants to participate as a shareholder needs to do the same. There are other ways to compensate those who give their time to help build the company. A free pass on ownership should not be one of them.

Proper legal representation

Mike and I always believed in getting the best legal counsel our budget could afford. We engaged mid-size national law firms to represent the business and the shareholders. Every business should engage a qualified law firm or attorney that understands a wide range of relevant legal issues when considering a partnership.

Sound legal representation protects the company and the partners, as well as the shareholders. We had shareholder agreements, and if there was a promissory note, the appropriate documentation was drawn up. Once obligations for promissory notes were met, we issued actual stock certificates.

Beyond the shareholder agreements, engaging a law firm to represent the business is a necessary part of running the day-to-day activities every small business encounters. We recorded board meeting notes and sent them to our law firm so they could be included in our corporate records. We were reluctant to enter any formal contractual relationships—with clients, employees, or contractors—without our attorneys ensuring that we were compliant and protected.

Perhaps we were overly cautious. We are, unfortunately, in a litigious business environment, so making sure we did everything we could from a legal perspective was all part of owning and running a successful enterprise.

13 | SEXISM AND THE FEMALE ENTREPRENEUR

■ ■ ■ ■ ■

"There is a special place in hell
for women who don't help other women."
Madeleine Albright

■ ■ ■ ■ ■

Over the years, I have run into various forms of sexism, whether in the form of outright discrimination, or men behaving badly, or because I chose not to have children. Sexism is the discriminatory or abusive behavior towards members of the opposite sex. Sexism can also be a result of complacency and insensitivity. There are many times when women in business blindly accept it or are indifferent to it.

In Sheryl Sandberg's book, *Lean In*, she addresses this very issue:

> One stumbling block is that many people
> believe that the workplace is largely a
> meritocracy, which means we look at

individuals, not groups, and determine that differences in outcomes must be based on merit, not gender. Men at the top are often unaware of the benefits they enjoy simply because they're men, and this can make them blind to the disadvantages associated with being a woman. Women lower down also believe that men at the top are entitled to be there, so they try to play by the rules and work harder to advance rather than raise questions or voice concerns about the possibility of bias. As a result, everyone becomes complicit in perpetuating an unjust system.

For most of my career, I worked with men who were open to the success of women in business. My male partners had children—all daughters—and wives or significant others in the workforce. I believe this contributed to their sensitivity towards the women who worked for us.

Many of my clients had women in powerful corporate roles as well, and some of them worked directly with us. As my company grew and we took on larger accounts, this dynamic shifted. We worked with mostly male clients in majority male-run organizations. Our agency expertise grew in the business-to-business area and often we engaged with companies where more men than women were in charge.

The account management, creative, and media leadership in the ad agency business has been historically male. The tide began to shift in the 1980s, when many of the account management and media groups consisted of a growing pool of young women. This was not necessarily true of the creative staff in ad agencies around the country (and the world), where it is still primarily male.

When our national trade organization appointed a woman president, Nancy Hill, for the first time in its 100+ year history, the women in our industry were thrilled. In a conversation I had with Nancy when she came to Atlanta to visit the member agencies, she told me that she asked the team at the association's headquarters in New York to remove the photos of all the past chairmen. "I had them take down the wall of white men," she said. Those photographs were a constant reminder of the lack of diversity our trade organization was unknowingly perpetuating.

Handling blatant sexism

As a female businessperson, sometimes sexism is blatant and sometimes it is subtle. There are some professional women who see it everywhere. I was so focused on moving the company ahead that I didn't notice it. I took mental note of the instances, but just as quickly moved on from them.

In a 2007 article for *Entrepreneur* magazine titled "Successful Communications Between the Sexes," Patti Simone offers the following sound advice for women faced with sexism:

- **Try not to take it personally.** Instead of getting ruffled feathers, stay focused and forward thinking. Count to 10, put a smile on your face, and move on. Try to devote your energy to what you need to do during the meeting or networking event, voicing your frustrations to a trusted peer after the fact.

- **Silence is sometimes the most effective weapon.** Cloddish behavior will always be around, no matter how far up the ladder you go. By not creating a scene, you can actually win.

- **Take charge.** Since you're running your own show, you can choose whom to do business with and whom to circumvent entirely.

- **Inform the clueless as necessary.** Lots of times, words tumble out before the person considers their potential impact. While, sadly, sometimes this is done on purpose, there are scads of situations when it's an accident. When you find you need to deal with inappropriate behavior or comments, approach things directly and swiftly, and with tact.

■ ■ ■ ■ ■

"Sexism is all about the power play. When you rise in power in the law firm, men become threatened by a strong woman partner, so their attitudes change."
A. Lizz Patrick, Founder, Patrick Law Group

■ ■ ■ ■ ■

Men behaving badly

When I started my business, I had more than a few encounters with flirtatious men. Many of these men never acted on their flirtations, but a few tried.

Flirting is one thing, men coming on too strong and expecting something else is quite another. When The Kilgannon Group opened its doors, my staff was comprised of mostly young, attractive women. Often, they encountered men who would overtly flirt. Fortunately, the women were successful in working around it. One staff member, however, complained that a vendor was coming on too strong. I had no tolerance for this behavior. We stopped working with his company.

Here are some of the ways I've encountered sexism:

- **No filter.** There were times when male clients or colleagues said something inappropriate regarding a female body part or a suggestive piece of clothing. Or worse, they lapsed into "frat boy" be-havior. At a dinner with one client and his invest-ment firm in New York City, the drinking got a little out of hand. There was a group of 10 men and two women at the table. The men clearly had no sense of filtering their words or behavior in the presence of women during a dinner that followed the meeting. Dumbfounded, I sat there with a weak smile on my face, all the while thinking, "I've got to get out of here!"

- **Inappropriate behavior.** I have been on many business trips with male clients and staff. On occa-sion, some men I traveled with seemed to think there might be opportunities beyond business. They might phone me late in the evening, when I was in my hotel room, to ask me to join them at the bar in the hotel lobby. Then there is the place of business where women do not typically conduct business. A friend of mine was contemplating the sale of her firm to one of her strategic partners. It would have been a great deal for her, save for a few things, one of which was this male business owner often brought his clients and prospects to adult-themed nightclubs. It was in this environ-ment where many deals were actually consum-mated. I was so naïve that I didn't realize this kind of thing even existed in this day and age. Apparently, this is a more common practice than most admit to.

- **Sexist women.** Believe it or not, many women do not like the idea of working for another woman. Somewhere along the line, women bosses got a terrible rap for being bitchy (the male equivalent is tough). Sexist women, in my opinion, are more difficult to manage than sexist men because they are always on the defensive. In all my years as an entrepreneur, there have been several women on my staff who overtly refused to deal directly with me and preferred to work with the men in my office.

Gender roles

What is acceptable for the roles women play versus men? Depending on the part of the country and the profession, women are telling new and exciting stories about their place in the professional world. But there are still stereotypes women have to overcome.

Many female entrepreneurs run into sexism in competitive bidding situations. My friend Mitzi Moore, Owner and President of Sundial Plumbing, told me of her attempts to win bids from foreign builders. "There are often cultural issues from male foreign-born builders. They will not deal with a woman business owner," she said. She also noted that there are credibility issues surrounding her position as owner and president of a plumbing company. "Often, people think there must be a man behind the business, such as my husband or father. I couldn't possibly be the one running the business."

I echo this last sentiment by Mitzi. I've had experiences when people would call my company asking for Mr. Kilgannon. When our receptionist would tell them that Mrs. Kilgannon is the one in charge, there was always an awkward pause. I have run into many situations where vendors or prospects asked the same question of me that they asked of Mitzi. Who was the man in my life who was really running the company?

A senior communications executive once recounted a story to me. She was participating in a business peer-to-peer meeting of 15 entrepreneurs; she was the only woman in attendance. The usual facilitator was out, and another facilitator agreed to help. After the speaker's session, this substitute facilitator singled her out, asking, "Would you mind recording our notes for this meeting?" She said the room fell silent as the other participants looked down at their notes to avoid the awkwardness of the request. One of the men in the group spoke up and said, "I'll take the notes." My friend alluded to the fact that this substitute facilitator probably did not understand the dynamics of this group, so they all forgave him. However, years later, she still tells the story.

■ ■ ■ ■ ■

"Becoming an entrepreneur has freed me from the burden of sexism. Could be because I'm getting older. But I do believe sexism is alive and well, unfortunately."
A. Lizz Patrick, Founder, Patrick Law Group

■ ■ ■ ■ ■

In recent years, women have advanced professionally more than ever, but not without controversy or commentary. Think of Marissa Meyer. Shortly after being appointed the CEO of Yahoo!, it was made public that she was expecting. Investors, Wall Street, media, and other pundits commented on her pregnancy, debating the fate of the company while she was on maternity leave. Not much was written about her abilities to create a new future for the brand. Meyer is part of a multi-billion dollar, publicly traded enterprise. Yahoo! has the where-withal to sustain the absence of its CEO for a couple of months. However, Meyer was only gone for a few weeks, so it's likely she didn't miss a beat.

Men in large and small corporations seem to be perplexed about how women juggle family and business. As many know, success for a woman entrepreneur does not boil down to the choice between having a family and running a business. Many successful female entrepreneurs have figured that out. While at dinner with three other female entrepreneurs—two of them had children and the other did not—one woman commented, "I never saw myself not having children; I've always wanted them. I didn't see the business as an obstacle to having children, or having kids as an obstacle to the business."

I never thought of myself as a mother. I was driven by my career goals. When I married Bob, he and I were of the same mind; he didn't want children either. My family often questioned my decision, but in the end, they came to accept it.

As I saw things, the business was my child. I would nurture it, grow it, and see to its health and happiness. That was enough for me. As I entered my 40s, however, I did occasionally question that decision. All of my good friends were having children, and I often wondered if I was missing something. But as I grew older, that question was hushed after I encountered some health issues. Once they were resolved, I was back to caring for my business.

I have, and have always had, an admiration for working women—whether entrepreneurs or not—who have made the choice to have children while building a lucrative career. These women have multiple jobs and often have little time for themselves in their exciting adventure of raising a family. It just wasn't for me.

In my opinion, the jury is still out on the issue of acceptable male or female gender roles. I believe that future generations will change perceptions of the roles women or men should play in business. There has been a growing emphasis of late on women's roles in the sciences, technology, engineering, and math (STEM). I believe the more women are viewed as equally capable and able to contribute in these areas, the more level the playing field will become.

Sexism is an issue that women will always face. Women's annual salaries continue to lag behind men's. Progress is being made on that front, and the debate about pay equality is ongoing. More women are being appointed to boards of directors, although not as quickly as necessary. I believe we will see a change in attitude about women's abilities to lead at the very top companies. Women have proved that we can be effective and successful entrepreneurs.

14 | SUCCESSION

■ ■ ■ ■ ■

"Life moves on and so should we."
Spencer Johnson, *Who Moved My Cheese?*

■ ■ ■ ■ ■

When Mike Reineck and I became partners in the late 1990s, we discussed what we would need to do to grow the business so that it would become viable to sell. Prior to that, I day-dreamed about one of the larger local firms wanting to buy my company. But it was a pipe dream back then.

After 11 years in business, my partners, Rick McReynolds and Mike Reineck, and I reviewed my balance sheet, and it looked weak. When Rick decided to retire, and we were buying his company shares back, Mike and I decided this was a perfect opportunity to bring the balance sheet back to full health. This meant repairing elements of our financials, which required us to focus on the state of the working capital in the business. Mike saw the potential to turn it around.

At the end of each year, we left a substantial amount of

money in the company, rather than draw it out as compensation or distribution. Mike projected that the focus on rebuilding the weakness in some of our numbers would likely improve our balance sheet over a five-year period, as long as our existing revenue remained the same or increased. Continuous improvement was preferable.

Mike had been successful overseeing the sale of a few companies before joining my firm, so he had valuable knowledge about how a sale works, and he taught me the financial requirements. We were clear on the amount of revenue that would attract an outside buyer to express interest. But we worried about the distribution of our revenue. The agency needed to add more clients, so that revenue distribution would be balanced, not generated by only one or two clients. This way, if one of those clients decided to move on, we could survive.

By 2006, our revenue number and balance sheet were improving steadily. Mike and I were diligent about our pricing model, our operational and financial procedures, and our accounts receivable, so that our numbers continuously looked healthy. We approached the process of selling the company armed with solid financials to get the maximum dollar amount, thereby leaving us financially secure into our retirement. At that point, we began discussions with a mergers and acquisitions firm in New York that specialized in our industry. We retained them to help us identify possible buyers for our company.

Just as we hit our stride in beginning succession planning, the Great Recession of 2008 hit. I remember having an out-of-body experience as I watched the stock market plummet hundreds of points for days at a time in the fall of 2008. All I could think about was how we were going to survive this.

2009 was a very dark year for my business. We lost 50 percent of our revenue due to client business closings and severe budget cutbacks. As a result, we had to reduce our staff, take salary cuts, remove our 401(k) matches, freeze salary increases, and initiate a hiring freeze. It was dismal. The good thing is that we had been fiscally responsible for the previous seven years, in preparation for a possible sale, enabling us to rely on our healthy balance sheet to keep the business running. But the plummeting morale that enveloped the country found a home at The Kilgannon Group. The news media ran frequent stories of people who had lost everything as a result of the economy. Our remaining staff was grateful to have a job.

In 2010, we were determined to rebuild. We had to restore the lost revenue we experienced in 2009. Our team was on board to be more aggressive in our outbound marketing. Social media was emerging as the way to communicate for many organizations. We had to get involved. We were an advertising agency, after all. At the same time, Mike began discussions with an ad agency in our region that was interested in expanding to the Atlanta market. By this time, our discussions with the M&A firm in New York had come to a screeching halt. Our numbers were too weak to present to any interested firm. Not that there were any firms interested in acquiring other companies during this time; there wasn't a lot happening in mergers in our industry on a national scale.

The recession hit our local competitors as hard as it hit us. A couple of them approached us about the possibility of a merger. Although we considered it, we had the added burden of a long-term office lease, which made a deal unattractive to our local potential merger partners.

We were back in discussions with the ad agency from out of town. This discussion began in 2010. Mike and I had a couple of meetings with the four partners at the other firm. As with many initial meetings, everyone was polite and seemed to get along. The sale was still a distant reality, so we let further discussions linger, although there were some brief conversations between their CEO and Mike when they ran into each other at conferences.

We barely kept our head above water. We initiated outbound marketing programs: blogging, social media, and e-mail marketing, and sought to improve networking opportunities. Neither outbound approach worked on its own, but the combination got us more opportunities to pitch business. We tried our best to adapt to the new reality.

I was weary. I lost heart, and it became evident to those around me. Every now and then, I got a surge of energy and hunkered down, but the hunger with which I founded the business nearly 25 years earlier was no longer there. I knew the best I could do for the company, my staff, and ultimately myself, was to secure all of our futures and sell.

In time, the company from out of town showed increased interest in us. I believe they seized an opportunity: we lost our creative leader and they had one. In addition, our financial acumen was stronger than theirs. From all perspectives, the merger made mutual sense; if we joined forces, two of our weaknesses could be addressed. An added bonus was that our onerous lease obligation was not an issue for this company since they were not in the Atlanta market and would have use of the office space.

From mid-2011 through the end of the year, we were in negotiations with them about merging. This process never sat well with me, as I wasn't sure this was the right move. Although I liked the CEO and the creative director, there were two other partners I did not care for. In addition, there were no women in senior management. I would be the only female partner, with a diminished ownership percentage.

I knew that once this deal was done, I would be out within a short period of time. The terms of the transaction were decent, and we closed the deal in early 2012. At the end of the day, everything we worked for, we achieved. The firm that acquired us kept the company I founded intact, for the most part. There were no client conflicts and limited staff redundancies, and both parties found a solution for their challenges. Theirs was to expand, ours was succession and to move to the next chapter of our careers.

So was this the worst that could happen? No, because it was in the plan all along. Could it have gone down better than it did? Probably. I made some poor decisions with the deal, but also some very sound ones. I made sure that I had the very best legal representation for the corporate end of the transaction and for the employment side. I traded the name of my company for the name of the acquiring one. Neither of us wanted it any other way. They needed to establish their name in a new market, and I wanted the name of my company retired upon closing. We had a great run as a business for 25 years. It was okay to move on.

At the end of a successful 25-year career as an entrepreneur, I am now on to the next chapter. I left the merged company after one year. Although I miss some of the people, I don't miss the business. I remain close to the many friends I made. I am very proud of what I built and the reputation for excellence we achieved.

Would I do it again? You bet. After all ... what's the worst that could happen?

■ ■ ■ ■ ■

"I'm not retiring; I'm rewiring!"
Rena Kilgannon

■ ■ ■ ■ ■

To learn more about Rena, visit www.renakilgannon.com

ABOUT THE AUTHOR

Rena Kilgannon was born and raised in the New York City area. She began her career in the textbook and professional book publishing industry at McGraw-Hill Book Company and Xerox Publishing Company. Upon her move to Atlanta in 1981, she began work for the advertising agency, Cargill, Wilson & Acree where she served as Vice President of direct marketing and public relations. This evolved into starting her own agency in 1988, Kilgannon, Inc. where she served as President and CEO. Following the successful sale of her company in 2012, she now runs Kilgannon Group, LLC, a marketing and small business consulting firm.

For her efforts to date, she's been profiled in Business-to-Business Magazine as a Woman of Excellence, and Working Women Magazine for an entrepreneurial excellence award. The American Advertising Federation recognized her in 2008 with the Silver Medal Award. Rena has been a guest lecturer in many MBA and undergraduate programs for Emory University, Georgia State University, and Kennesaw State University.

Rena has served on various non-profit boards, including Partnership Against Domestic Violence, Junior Achievement of Georgia, Hands on Atlanta, and the executive leadership team for the American Heart Association's Go Red for Women event. She currently serves on the board of the Georgia Chapter of the

Multiple Sclerosis Society. She is a graduate of the Leadership Atlanta Class of 2010.

Rena attended Fordham University in New York where she studied marketing management.

MEET THE EXPERTS

Interview with Ellen Dracos Lemming
President, Dracos-Lemming, LLC

Ellen Dracos Lemming is a lifelong strategic marketer with expertise in branding, strategy, planning, and assessment. A graduate of Duke University, Ellen began her career on Madison Avenue leading iconic consumer brands within advertising agencies such as J. Walter Thompson and Wells Rich Greene. Graduating from agency side to corporate marketing roles, Ellen has been the chief brand officer for industry leaders such as The Home Depot, Kaplan Educational Centers, and Emory University. She runs a successful and growing strategic branding and marketing consultancy in Atlanta. Ellen divides her precious free time between serving key philanthropic organizations, mentoring women, traveling with her husband, and perfecting her macro-photography.

How long have you had your own business? What led to the founding of your business?

I've been in business since March of 2007. I was with The Home Depot for seven years, and after eight bosses in that period of time, I decided to move on. I went to Emory University as their Vice President of Marketing. Shortly after

I arrived, the person who hired me was fired. I learned pretty quickly that the pace of academia was not for me. Plus, I was tired of working for male bosses and making them rich! If I was going to work hard, I wanted to keep the rewards for myself. And I wanted more control over my time.

Was owning a business in the master plan for your career?
No. I was in the corporate world for 22 years. My father advised me, early on, that I should work for large corporations—especially those who are the leading companies in their industries.

What was your biggest fear when you started the business?
Can I sell? I was always concerned that no one would hire me. But shortly after I started the business, I got my first assignment. I didn't know if the pricing was right. I underpriced projects so that I could grow my client list.

What's your fear now?
I fear that someone could ruin my personal brand reputation. Whether it is a client or employee saying something negative.

One topic of the book is to ask for what you want. When you saw something you wanted, how did you go after it?
When I started my business, I asked myself, "What's the worst thing that could happen? I go back to work for old white guys?"

Are you risk-averse or a risk taker?
I take calculated risks. I would not say I am fearless, but I am adventuresome. Starting a company was a financial risk, but because I was married and my husband did well financially, I was fortunate enough to have that financial cushion.

I probably would not have tried if I did not have that to fall back on.

Fear: in Sheryl Sandberg's book, *Lean In*, she mentions that women need to put aside their fears and move forward. What do you think about women's propensity towards fear?

I think women operate under the assumption that it is a man's world. Women start out handicapped. That subconscious, subversive outlook holds women back. Fear of not being good enough, and fear of being known as the stereotypical bitch. I've never had a female figure I aspired to be like in business. There is a saying, "Feel the fear and do it anyway." I believe in that. I've had moments of self-doubt, but it never held me back.

What about consequences, good and bad?

No one is going to die if my business goes under; I'll reinvent myself. I worry about my teammates, though. It's not just about me anymore. Now, it's about my associates and their families.

What are your hopes for the business moving forward?

I hope that our work makes a difference for the companies we work for. I hope we provide actionable insights they can implement.

What advice would you give young women who are thinking of starting their own business?

You don't need a master plan.

Interview with Mitzi Moore
President, Sundial Plumbing

Mitzi Moore is the president of Sundial Plumbing Services, a full-service plumbing contractor serving residential and commercial clients. Sundial is the largest female-owned Plumbing Contractor in Georgia and has won numerous national and local awards.

Mitzi earned a bachelor of business management degree with a minor in finance from Georgia Southern University and attended the master's program for middle childhood education at Kennesaw State University. She also holds a Master Class II Unrestricted Plumbing License, Class III Boiler Certification, Level IA in Water Conservation and Soil Erosion Certification, and her Georgia Residential and Light Commercial Contractors License, among numerous other state and OSHA certifications.

Mitzi serves on numerous professional boards. Her passion is community philanthropy advocacy for organizations focused on children, education, and vocation, as well as humanitarian and equality efforts.

Mitzi lives in Marietta, GA with her husband, Richard, and has two adult children. She enjoys reading, genealogy, traveling, and long walks with her husband and dog, Sonnet.

How did you get started in this business?

I was a homemaker with two children. I was going through a very tough divorce. I was a victim of domestic violence and undoing the marriage was very difficult. It was apparent that I needed a job, but I was limited in that I had two young children to care for. My dad had a plumbing company, and he offered me a job in his office. I fell in love with the business, and I told my dad that I wanted to stay with the company. He insisted I get my plumbing license, so I would know good plumbing from bad. I had to learn from the best plumbers we had.

Your business is in a male-dominated field. Do you feel you have to overcome being a woman in the business?

There are huge credibility issues. Often people think there must be a man behind the business, such as my husband or my father. I couldn't possibly be the one running the business. There are also cultural issues from foreign-born builders who will not deal with a woman. As for a woman-owned business in this field, there are specific obstacles, such as discrimination. Occasionally, I will meet someone who is in awe of what I do, and that is validating.

Tell me about doubts or fears you had once you decided to move forward.

I wondered if I could do it. It's difficult and hard work. Once I got through the learning process, I gained confidence. I found the business side of running the company very challenging. It's like running a manufacturing business. Once I understood the trade part, I had to learn the complications of running the day-to-day business. I was both afraid and challenged.

What advice do you have for young women entering a non-conventional business like plumbing?

Think about your values and what's important to you. Be introspective, using your values as a base. Always think that no matter if you are a file clerk or a plumbing apprentice, you are building your resume. Everything you do will have an impact.

It is a blessing to be a woman in that you have to work harder. Also, be sure to understand the power of relationships and how to leverage them. Be open to all the connections you make and develop those relationships. Meet as many people as you can.

Interview with A. Lizz Patrick
Founder, Patrick Law Group, Atlanta, Georgia

A. Elizabeth ("Lizz") Patrick is the founder of Patrick Law Group, LLC, a women-owned law firm focused on preparing and negotiating construction, technology, outsourcing, and other commercial contracts for corporations. Prior to starting Patrick Law Group, Lizz was a partner in the Real Estate and Construction Groups at two AM Law 100 Law Firms located in Atlanta, and at one of those firms, she served as the Practice Group Leader.

Lizz received her undergraduate degree from the University of Georgia in 1985, and her law degree from Tulane University School of Law in 1988. She graduated fifth in her class and served as a member of the Tulane Law Review.

In recognition of her outstanding legal ability and experience, Lizz has been named one of the Best Lawyers in America, and has been recognized in Chambers U.S.A., Georgia Legal Elite, and International Who's Who of Construction Lawyers. She has also been selected as a Georgia Super Lawyer from 2004–2014, and as one of the Top 50 Female Super Lawyers. She has achieved Martindale-Hubbell''s highest rating of AV for legal ability and ethical standards. She is a frequent speaker and publisher.

You started your own firm several years ago. What were your plans to grow the business in the start-up phase?

I was always worried about the growth of the business. What was going to happen six months from now when my current work was wrapping up? I was always concerned about what was in the pipeline. I ended up going to my network of business people. Throughout my career, I had always mentored young women, and many of these women ended up on the client side. I always maintained my relationship with them, so I went to them and told them my philosophy, and many of them either gave me business or referred me.

Where has it not worked out? What happened when you didn't get what you wanted?

When I realized that I was alone as an entrepreneur, I built on my network. I joined a peer-to-peer group of entrepreneurs. I stayed involved with my network, and I was persistent with everything I did, whether it was business development or running the business effectively. If something did not work out for me—when I did not win business for example—I quickly moved on and deliberately stayed in touch with the client in the hopes of getting the next project.

What has been the effect of entrepreneurship on your personal life?

Early in my career, I was married and that marriage didn't work out. When I decided to start my own business, I was well into my second marriage with someone who supported my vision for where this business could go. My husband offered me the support I needed.

Interview with Stacy Williams
President, Prominent Placement, Inc.

Stacy Williams began doing search engine optimization (SEO) in 1998. She founded Prominent Placement, Inc. (PPI), a full-service, award-winning Atlanta search engine marketing firm, in 2001. Prior to her establishment of Prominent Placement, Stacy's career spanned both coasts, serving at advertising agencies in both Los Angeles and Atlanta.

A graduate of the University of California at Berkeley's Haas School, she received a B.S. in business administration, with an emphasis in marketing. Stacy also received an M.A. in communications management from the University of Southern California's Annenberg School.

Stacy is sought after nationwide as a speaker about search engine marketing, and is frequently published on the subject. She is a NewsCertified Exchange Expert. She was a founding member of SEMPO Atlanta, a local chapter of the global Search Engine Marketing Professional Organization, and served as its president in 2012. Stacy was named Search Engine Marketer of the Year for 2013 by the Technology Association of Georgia.

What led to the founding of your business? Was there a specific trigger point?

I worked for a small ad agency for nine years. During my time there, I had two babies and eventually worked part-time. I was doing the same thing for so long, I was getting bored. Plus, I was feeling itchy. I no longer felt like I belonged there. Sometimes I was on the owner's good side, sometimes on her bad side. I liken it to being in the land of the misfit toys!

I attended a conference in my area of specialty, search marketing, and I noticed that many of the attendees ran their own businesses, and that really appealed to me. If I did that, I thought, then I could do what I wanted, and this was something I could be passionate about. I wanted to feel like I could live up to my full potential.

Plus, I could take the risk of owning my own business because my husband was earning a six-figure income at the time. And I could work from home for four hours per day, and at the same time, be there for my babies.

Was there something you wanted for the business, but may not have attained? Did you eventually get it?
I wanted to be well-known and respected. I gave presentations to potential clients and ad agencies and began to gain their respect.

Did you have advisors? What type of advisors did you seek out?
At first I did not seek advisors. After I ran the company for three years, I attended a class called Fast Track that was offered by the Small Business Administration. At this class I learned how to write a business plan and how to run an effective small business.

I also learned about the Vistage® organization and became a member of a Vistage® group. I get great advice from my Vistage® chairman as well as the group members. I hired an outside advisor once, which did not end up well. He led me down the wrong road. But fortunately, I recovered.

Are you risk averse?
I am a low-risk person. I took baby steps in the beginning, and then I started to build momentum. I am a people-pleaser; I want everyone to like me. Plus, I am a consensus builder.

What is your version of "what's the worst that could happen?"

I don't prepare (financial) projections enough, and that worries me. It takes me too long to hire people, and I am sometimes very impulsive. I am an open book, and sometimes I tell people too much. I'm working on that.

BIBLIOGRAPHY

Sindell, Thuy, Ph.D, and Milo Sindell, M.S. "How to Pick an Executive Coach." Psychology Today (2012): n. pag. Web. 13 Aug. 2012. <psychologytoday.com>.

Wagner, Eric. "Seven Traits of Incredibly Successful Entrepreneurs." Forbes Magazine (2012): n. pag. www.forbes.com. Forbes, June 2012. Web.09. N. pag. Print.

Roché, Joyce. "10 Ways to Overcome Imposter Syndrome." Web log post. Http://blog.vistage.com. Vistage® Organization, 22 July 2013. Web. <www.vistage.com>.

Sandberg, Sheryl. *Lean In: Women, Work, and the Will to Lead.* New York: Alfred A. Knopf, 2013. 150. Print.

Daley, Jason. "Are Entrepreneurs Born or Made?" Entrepreneur Magazine (2013): n. pag. Www.entrepreneur.com. Entrepreneur Magazine, 19 Sept. 2013. Web. <www.entrepreneur.com>.

Scheidies, Nick. "Six Traits All Entrepreneurs Secretly Have in Common." Www.incomediary.com. Income Diary, 2012. Web. <www.incomediary.com>.

Tice, Carol. "Why Women Business Owners Feel More Successful." Web log post. http://www.entrepreneur.com/blog. Entrepreneur Magazine, 6 Apr. 2012. Web. www.entrepreneur.com>.

Amorós, José Ernesto Amorós, Niels Bosma, and Global Entrepreneurship Research Association. Global Entrepreneurship Monitor (GEM). Rep. no. ISBN: 978-1-939242-04-4. 15th ed. N.p.: Global Entrepreneurship Research Association, n.d. Print.

Simone, Pattie. "Successful Communications Between the Sexes." *Entrepreneur Magazine* (2007): n. pag. Print.

RESOURCES

I could fill out pages and pages of online and offline resources available for entrepreneurs, male or female. Here are a few to get you started:

Women Business Owner's Resources

Women's Business Enterprise National Council (WBENC)
Founded in 1997, WBENC is the largest third-party certifier of businesses owned, controlled, and operated by women in the United States. WBENC provides and manages the development, enforcement, and implementation of its world-class certification, which is nationally accepted by thousands of major corporations and a select group of government entities. Visit www.wbenc.com.

National Women Business Owners Corporation (NWBOC)
Created in 1995, NWBOC was established to increase competition for corporate and government contracts through implementation of a national certification program for women business owners. Visit www.nwboc.org.

National Association of Women Business Owners (NAWBO)

Founded in 1975, NAWBO is the unified voice of America's more than 10 million women-owned businesses representing the fastest growing segment of the economy. NAWBO is the only dues-based organization representing the interests of all women entrepreneurs across all industries, and boasts over 5000 members and 60 chapters across the country. Visit www.nawbo.org.

Astia

Founded in 1999 in Silicon Valley, Astia is an innovative global not-for-profit organization that connects entrepreneurs to investors, industry leaders, advisors, and service providers encircling the entrepreneur with a comprehensive value-ad network. Visit www.astia.org.

National Women's Business Council (NWBC)

The National Women's Business Council is a bipartisan federal government council created to serve as an independent source of advice and counsel to the President, Congress, and the U.S. Small Business Administration on economic issues of importance to women business owners. Members of the Council are prominent women business owners and leaders of women's business organizations. For more information about the Council, its mission and activities, visit www.nwbc.gov.

Women Impacting Public Policy (WIPP)

Women Impacting Public Policy is a national group comprising over half a million members. The non-profit organization is the public policy voice for 49 national Women in Business groups and is the voice for women in business in our nation's capital. WIPP strengthens its members' sphere of influence in the legislative process, creates economic opportunities for members, and builds alliances with other small business organizations. Visit www.wipp.org.

Publications

Forbes: www.forbes.com

Entrepreneur: www.entrepreneur.com

The Huffington Post: www.huffingtonpost.com

Peer-to-peer groups

Vistage®

Since 1957, Vistage has made a difference by bringing together groups of successful executives across a broad array of industries. The goal: more success. Each group is designed to help members help each other improve their businesses and their lives. Visit www.vistage.com.

CEO Focus

CEO Focus is a peer consulting group of company presidents and CEOs from various industries. In group meetings, work is done on business issues confronting members. By creating an informal board of advisors, members improve their company performance. Visit www.ceofocus.com.

Chief Executive Network (CEN)

CEN helps chief executives improve their effectiveness and gain competitive advantage. Members are placed in industry-specific, revenue compatible, non-competing groups facilitated by trained experts to share innovative ideas, solve specific problems, and uncover best practices. Visit www.chiefexecutivenetwork.com.

Entrepreneurial websites for women

The Boss Network: A community of entrepreneurial women who support each other through conversation and online and event-based networking, the BOSS network makes minority business owners a priority. www.thebossnetwork.org.

The Chic CEO: For women with the entrepreneur bug, the advice this site delivers covers everything from idea-generation to patents and copyrights to the pros and cons of buying a franchise. Great design and a clever blog round out the experience for those thinking about entrepreneurship or those who have already launched a startup. www.chic-ceo.com

The Founding Moms: This site provides a networking community for mompreneurs and work-at-home moms in North America, Australia, and the United Kingdom. www.foundingmoms.com.

Ladies Who Launch: This active and engaging site for female entrepreneurs provides resources for starting, building, and running a business, including engaging video interviews with top tier entrepreneurs and networking events. www.theladieswholaunch.org.

Count Me In: Count Me In for Women's Economic Independence is the leading national not-for-profit provider of resources, business education, and community support for women entrepreneurs seeking to grow micro-businesses into million dollar enterprises. www.countmein.com.

Mom Invented: Tamara Monosoff launched this online community for entrepreneurial moms. It supports and inspires women inventors with business advice and product licensing opportunities. www.mominvented.com.

She Takes on the World: One of the 20 best marketing and social media blogs by women, She Takes On The World is an award-winning business and lifestyle blog for women. www.shetakesontheworld.com.

StartUp Princess: A resource for female entrepreneurs, by female entrepreneurs, providing education, encouragement, and networking opportunities. www.startupprincess.com.

Women Entrepreneurs: The female arm of Entrepreneur.com, this site is a resource for current and aspiring women business owners, featuring in-depth profiles of success stories as well as up-to-date advice on funding. www.entrepreneur.com/women.

Books

The Accidental Entrepreneur: The 50 Things I Wish Someone Had Told Me About Starting a Business, by Susan Urquhart-Brown.

Business Insider has a list of books every entrepreneur should read. These are the standard must-read business books like Dale Carnegie's *How to Win Friends and Influence People* and Jim Collins's *From Good to Great.* www.businessinsider.com/best-business-books-for-entrepreneurs-2013-5.

Amazon.com has a list of Good Books for New Female Entrepreneurs *The Girls Guide to Starting Your Own Business, Harvard Business Review on Women in Business,* and *Careerpreneurs* are among the titles recommended. www.amazon.com.

Entreprenista has a list of must reads for women entrepreneurs. Their recommended reading list includes *The Fire Starter Sessions, Daring Greatly,* and *The Barefoot Executive.*

http://entreprenista.com/blog/business-sense/10-amazing-must-read-books-for-women-entrepreneurs.